Field Guide to

TOOLS

How to Identify and Use Virtually Every Tool at the Hardware Store

By John Kelsey

QUIRK BOOKS

PHILADELPHIA

DISCLAIMER

The world of tools is very large. While we've taken care to represent popular and useful tools for handypersons, the author and publisher cannot guarantee that this guide addresses every possible tool. Safety is of utmost importance when using tools: Be sure to employ the proper safety gear. The author and publisher are not liable for any use or misuse of tools by the reader.

Copyright © 2004 by Quirk Productions, Inc.
All rights reserved. No part of this book may be reproduced in any form without written permission from the publisher.

Library of Congress Cataloging in Publication Number: 2004103016

ISBN: 1-931686-79-3

Printed in Singapore

Typeset in Adobe Garamond, Franklin Gothic, and Impact

Designed by Karen Onorato
Edited by Erin Slonaker
Photographs by John Kelsey
Illustrations by Clarke Barre

All photographs copyright © 2004 by Quirk Productions, Inc.

Distributed in North America by Chronicle Books
85 Second Street
San Francisco, CA 94105

10 9 8 7 6 5 4 3 2 1

Quirk Books
215 Church Street
Philadelphia, PA 19106
www.quirkbooks.com

Contents

IV. GARDEN AND YARD

VII. WOODWORKING

VIII. FASTENERS

IX. PLUMBING

X. MECHANICAL AND AUTOMOTIVE

Introduction

Tools extend the hands. You already know what your soft hands can accomplish in easy materials such as paper or cookie dough. You can do the same things in big and tough materials such as earth, wood, and metal when you make use of tools. You might be a person who's always had other priorities, but you're finding you have a need for a specific tool from time to time. You might encounter tools almost anywhere—in a store or home workshop, on a truck, on the street, or at your job. Knowing what they are called and what they are meant to do is the first step, and that's one objective of this book.

When I sat down to write this guide, I was surprised to discover that I already had most of this stuff. The tools and machines were scattered throughout two garages and a garden shed—some new, some old, and some worn out. When I went looking, I found the same general assortment at the homes of friends and neighbors. What I mean is, this is not the collection of some tool-crazed nut. It's just a sampling of what handypersons are likely to acquire once they come to find satisfaction in making things and maintaining the homestead.

I'd like to encourage you to try the tools out for yourself. Learn how they feel and work, so you can choose the ones that promise to be of help with your own endeavors. That's when the real fun begins.

I. Shop Safety

A little safety consciousness goes a long way. Train yourself to think about safety before beginning to work. You'll find it is easy, and also more comfortable, to anticipate hazards and take precautions. Put on work boots, work gloves, safety goggles, and hearing protection. Think about where you'll apply force and what's likely to ensue. And never drive a tool toward your hand or any other part of your body.

---

1. **CLAMP**

General Description:
A heavy, G-shaped apparatus that can be tightened on objects that fit between its opposed jaws. The back of the G consists of a heavy iron bar with a fixed jaw at one end facing an adjustable jaw that slides along the bar. There's a stout wooden handle on the sliding part. Turning the handle tightens the clamp screw, squeezing the distance between the jaws and, with it, the object you placed in between.

Habitat:
Builder's toolbox, woodworker's shop, and tradesman's truck. Sold by home centers and hardware stores.

Primary Uses:
Holding the workpiece tight on the workbench, or onto another part of the job, so the operator has both hands available for applying other tools. Holding

parts together while glue dries. Assembling jigs for holding the workpiece in position for such machine operations as sawing, routing, or drilling. Fastening a worktable atop temporary supports on the job site.

Clamps are safety devices because injuries are almost inevitable when the handyperson unthinkingly holds the job in one hand while driving a tool with the other. Obeying Murphy's Law (whatever can go wrong will), when the tool slips, it smashes, slices, or chews into the hand that was holding the work. To avoid this, acquire the habit of clamping whatever you're working on to something solid.

Secondary Uses:	Quickly installing a sign, flag, or banner on a deck or railing. Creating a card-table barrier across a stairwell to keep a baby from tumbling down (use three or four clamps with handles oriented away from the baby). Pressing garlic, gravlax, or flowers. Not good for temporarily reattaching car parts because motor vibration is liable to wiggle the clamp loose (use locking pliers, page 259).
Operating Principle:	The screw. Turning the handle tightens the movable jaw of the clamp onto the workpiece. The bigger the screw, the tighter the squeeze. Some light-duty clamps operate with a lever and cam mechanism.
Variations:	Clamps vary in heft, jaw opening, and tightening mechanism. Match heft to the task at hand, and

when in doubt get a bigger one. Pipe and bar clamps can squeeze doors, windows, and whole pieces of furniture together so screws can be driven and glue can dry. Spring clamps work like spring clothespins. Cabinetmaker's clamps have two big, flat wooden jaws and two opposed screw-thread handles; their jaws can be tightened absolutely parallel, or not parallel, as suits the job. Picture-frame clamps hold two mitered moldings together for nailing. Some clamps have reversible jaws for pushing assemblies apart.

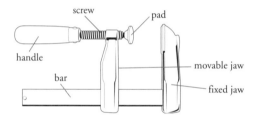

How to Use: 1. **Choose clamps of suitable heft and jaw opening.**

2. **Open the clamp and plant the fixed jaw on the workpiece. If the surface is delicate, protect it with smooth blocks of wood.**

3. **Hold the fixed jaw in place while you bring the movable jaw onto the workpiece.**

4. **Twist or squeeze the handle (depending on clamp**

style) to create a firm but not crushing grip.

5.　**If anything moves, add a second clamp.**

Tool-Kit
Minimum:

You can never have too many clamps.

2. 　**DUST MASK**

General
Description:

A paper or fabric hemisphere or cup about the size of your closed fist. An elastic strip or headband is fastened to opposite points on the rim of the hemisphere. A thin, finger-length strip of shiny metal may be glued parallel to the rim. To fit the cup over your face, bend the metal strip to fit your nose inside.

Habitat:

Found among sanding and painting tools. Sold by paint stores, home centers, and hardware stores. The stiffness of the mask distinguishes it from hospital masks, which are soft. Dust masks are disposable.

Primary
Use:

When worn over the mouth and nose, the dust mask helps the worker avoid inhaling harmful airborne particles. Usually worn during such dust-producing activities as sanding wood, paint, or drywall compound. Regular dust masks are not effective against fumes and vapors, such as paint solvents and thinners, nor against disease-causing microbes.

Secondary Uses: When pressed inside a funnel, most dust masks will filter dissolved particles from liquids.

Operating Principle: The material is sufficiently porous to transmit air but, since the pores are smaller than most dust motes, not dust. To be effective, the rim of the mask should make a tight seal around the wearer's mouth and nose (not easily accomplished if the user has a beard).

Variations: Cartridge-style masks, which resemble military gas masks, can filter harmful fumes and vapors. Hospital-style face masks are effective against airborne dust.

How to Use: 1. **Choose a new dust mask whose packaging suggests it is appropriate for the dust you wish to avoid.**

2. **Fit the dust mask over your mouth and nose, with the elastic strip passing around your head. If there is a little metal strip, press it to a nice fit on the bridge of your nose.**

3. **Breathe normally through the mask while engaged in a dust-producing job. When done, remove and discard the mask.**

Tool-Kit Minimum: Disposable dust masks are cheap insurance—always keep a package in your toolbox.

3.   **FIRE EXTINGUISHER**

General
Description: *A red metal cylinder with a trigger handle on top and a short black hose hanging down.* A close look reveals a wire ring terminating in a long metal pin in a hole passing completely through the handle. Its small, round gauge is divided into two red sectors and a narrow green wedge.

Habitat: A fire extinguisher normally hangs waist-high on a quick-release mounting bracket near kitchen, laundry room, garage, and workroom exits. May also be found in hallways outside bedrooms or inside bedroom closets. Sold by hardware stores and home centers. The tank, trigger, and nozzle arrangement are characteristic; the red color is customary but some extinguishers are white or chrome.

Primary
Use: Putting out a small fire before it spreads and before the fire department arrives. An extinguisher may also help suppress flames along your exit route.

Operating
Principle: A harmless gas such as nitrogen or carbon dioxide, when compressed inside a metal cylinder and released through a nozzle, can propel foam or dry powder along with it. Most household extinguishers contain either sodium bicarbonate or ammonium phosphate, powdery chemicals that interfere with the runaway oxidation we see as a flame.

Variations: Small extinguishers have a nozzle in the handle, while larger ones have a flexible black hose the same length as the cylinder. According to the National Association for Fire Prevention, for home use choose an extinguisher with a minimum rating of 2-A:10-B:C, which means it will be effective on type A fires (ordinary combustibles such as paper, wood, and fabric), type B fires (flammable liquids such as cooking oil and gasoline), and type C fires (involving live electricity). Home extinguishers should be rated A:B:C on their labels; it's unwise to rely on B:C or A:B ratings. The numbers in the rating, while not exactly a measurement, do allow you to compare the effectiveness of various extinguishers, with higher being better.

Safety Note: Fire extinguishers can lose their charge of propellant and become ineffective. The little round gauge warns you: If the needle slips out of its green wedge, you must recharge or replace the extinguisher.

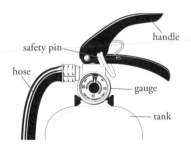

handle
safety pin
hose
gauge
tank

How to Use: 1.   **Call 911 and begin to evacuate the building.**

2.   **If you cannot position yourself between the flames and the exit from the building, do not attempt to fight the fire.**

3.   **Lift the extinguisher and pull the safety pin completely out of the handle.**

4.   **Aim the extinguisher's nozzle at the base or source of the flames and squeeze the handle to release the fire suppressant.**

5.   **Sweep the stream of fire suppressant from side to side across the base or source of the flames until the extinguisher is completely empty.**

6.   **Even if you put out the fire, do not cancel the 911 call. The fire department will want to confirm that the fire is indeed out.**

7.   **If the extinguisher does not put out the fire, immediately leave the building and wait outside for the fire department to arrive.**

8.   **As soon as the crisis is past, replace or refill the extinguisher and return it to the wall bracket.**

<table>
<tr><td>Tool-Kit
Minimum:</td><td>Install an extinguisher with a minimum rating of 2-A:10-B:C near the exit from your kitchen, another near the exit from your laundry room, another in your garage or home workshop, another in the closet or hallway near each group of bedrooms, and another in each of your automobiles.</td></tr>
</table>

4.   **GASOLINE CAN**

General
Description: *A sturdy red container with a top-mounted carrying handle, a fist-sized opening, and a stubby spout; both openings have screw-on lids.* Metal gasoline cans are tougher than plastic ones.

Habitat: Found in detached garages and toolsheds. Sold by home centers and auto parts stores. Distinguish red gas cans from blue kerosene cans by their color.

Primary
Use: Filling the fuel tanks of gasoline-powered equipment such as lawn mowers, leaf blowers, chain saws, snow throwers, and even cars. *Mad Max* and other petrol-powered postapocalypse road-warrior movies not withstanding, gasoline is perishable and may go bad within six months, so do not store more than you have an immediate need for.

Secondary
Uses: None. To avoid potentially disastrous mishaps, gas cans must not be used for anything other than gaso-

line, and gasoline must not be stored in anything other than a red gas can.

Variations: Gas cans range in size from 1 gallon (3.8 l, or about twice the size of your head) up to 5 gallons (19 l, or about the size of your torso). Some models have a long screw-on spout.

Safety Note: Because gasoline is volatile, flammable stuff, gas cans should not be stored in the house or attached garage, kept in the trunk of the car, or in the hot sun. Store the gas can in a detached garage or garden shed.

How to Use: 1.   **Bring the gas can to the power equipment, preferably outdoors.**

2.   **Open the filler cap on the equipment.**

3.   **Open the spout on the gas can.**

4.   **Loosen the larger filler lid on the can so air can enter, otherwise the gas will splash.**

5.   **Lift the can and position the spout over the equipment's gas inlet.**

6.   **Tilt the can so the gasoline flows into the equipment. Sometimes the can and the equipment are not compatible—a funnel (page 25) can make the connection.**

7.   **Put the can down flat. Replace the equipment's filler cap and close the can's two caps.**

Tool-Kit
Minimum:
If you have gasoline-powered machinery, you need a gasoline can.

5a–c.   **GLOVES**

General
Description:
Fabric, leather, latex, or vinyl coverings for the hands and wrists, shaped to separately enclose the thumb and each finger. Gloves are important safety tools worn to protect the skin from physical abrasion by tools and materials, or from chemical attack by solvents and cleaning solutions.

Habitat:
Toolbox, garage, workshop, or closet. Sold by hardware stores, drugstores, and home centers. Leather and fabric work gloves may be distinguished from

dress gloves by their heavier weight and inexact fit. Reusable latex gloves may be distinguished by their close fit, bright color (typically yellow, pink, or blue), and mid-forearm length. Disposable latex and vinyl gloves, which are sold in one configuration that fits either hand, are thin and translucent.

Primary Use:
Protecting the hands from physical or chemical damage. Force exerted on tool handles grinds equally on the hand that works the tool, causing blisters, cuts, and (eventually) self-protective calluses. Chemical solutions used for cleaning may cause dermatitis as they soak into the skin of the hands; some solvents, notably methyl alcohol, suck the moisture out of skin, while such solvents as auto degreaser, lacquer thinner, acetone, and ketone may also leach fat from your flesh (not a substitute for diet and exercise). Impermeable gloves made of vinyl or latex offer almost complete protection from chemicals and solvents. They also protect hands from becoming coated with paint and varnish.

Secondary Uses:
Keeping warm in winter. Vinyl and latex also offer protection from blood-borne diseases while performing first aid.

Variations:
Some work gloves are covered with plastic or rubber dots to improve their grip. Some are insulated for working outdoors in winter. Some are knit of Kevlar

yarn, which is tough enough to deflect sharp knives. Some people are allergic to latex and should therefore choose vinyl (or vice versa).

How to Use: 1.   **Choose a pair of work gloves that comfortably fit your hands and that have protective features appropriate to the task.**

2.   **Put the gloves on before you set to work.**

3.   **When you are done working, take the gloves off. If they are disposable, dispose of them. If they are reusable, wash them.**

Tool-Kit Minimum: One pair fabric or leather gloves, one pair regular rubber gloves, one package disposable vinyl gloves.

6.   **HEARING PROTECTORS**

General Description: *Two fist-sized cups, each the shape of an egg halved lengthwise, connected by an adjustable band and worn over the ears to prevent annoyance or damage from loud sound.* Each cup has a rim of soft material that conforms to the shape of the head.

Habitat: Found in garages or workshops near noisy electrical or gasoline-powered equipment. Sold by home centers and hardware stores.

Primary
Use:

Protecting the wearer from hearing damage by block-ing high-intensity sound energy from the tiny struc-tures inside the ear. High-intensity sound can perma-nently damage those tiny structures and cause partial deafness, with high-pitched sounds, such as children's laughter, being the first to go.

Secondary
Uses:

Protection while lingering near the woofers at a rock concert. Keeping ears warm in winter.

Variations:

Small earplugs made of expanding foam also work, as do motorcycle helmets with built-in earphones. Sound-canceling earphones meant to help air travelers sleep are insufficient protection against loud tools.

How to Use: 1.

Choose hearing protection that is rated for the inten-sity of sound you expect to encounter. Some hearing protectors are better for the high-pitched sound of electrical machinery while others are designed for the low-pitched growl of gasoline engines. Hearing pro-tectors vary greatly in their ability to block speech.

2.

Before switching on the source of noise, don the hearing protectors so that the soft sides of the cups completely cover each ear. Adjust the band connect-ing the ear cups so it comfortably fits over the top of your head, not around your neck or the back of your head. If you wish to wear a hat, put it on first, then make sure it is completely outside the ear cups.

3.   **Operate the noisy equipment as needed.**

4.   **Once you've turned off the noisy equipment, remove the hearing protectors. Store them where you can find them next time.**

Tool-Kit   One comfortable pair of hearing protectors for your-
Minimum: self, plus a spare pair for a guest.

7.   **POCKETKNIFE**

General   *A small, finger-length assembly consisting of a plastic*
Description: *and metal handle and one or more sharp steel blades*
            connected by pivots so that the blades fold out of and
            into the handle. The pocketknife, immortalized by the
            Swiss army, may be the most ubiquitous of tools.

Habitat: Trouser pocket, toolbox, or handbag. Sold by cutlers
            and hardware stores. Distinguish the pocketknife
            from other cutting implements by its small size and
            folding ability.

Primary   Cutting and slicing. The folding knife is truly a uni-
Uses: versally handy tool. Few handypersons would consider
            themselves fully dressed without a knife tucked into
            pocket or handbag—an essential accoutrement picked
            up each morning along with eyeglasses, wallet, and
            keys. While not strictly a safety device, a pocketknife

will make life easier and come in handy in the event of a genuine emergency.

Secondary Uses:
Cleaning fingernails. Opening taped cartons, plastic security packaging, and recalcitrant CD cases. Slicing salami on picnics. Making layout lines on wood, plastic, and metal. Removing fishhooks and cleaning fish. Cutting tangled laces. Making kindling out of scrap wood. Whittling small sticks smaller while rocking on the verandah.

Variations:
Many pocketknives have a locking mechanism so the blade can't fold on the operator's fingers. Some pocketknives approach jewelry in their intricate and precious detailing, which might include gold blade inlays, silver monograms, and mother-of-pearl handle facings. Some—notably the Swiss Army knife—sport a thicket of special-purpose blades and devices such as tweezers, a saw blade, a bottle opener, and a magnifying glass. The orchardist's pruning and grafting knife has a single curved blade with a sliding ferrule that locks it open.

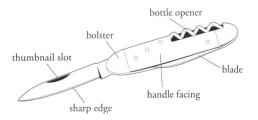

How to Use: 1. **Unfold the necessary tool by catching it in the thumbnail cutout.**

2. **Use the knife as required.**

3. **Fold the knife and put it back in your pocket.**

Tool-Kit Minimum: Shop for a little pocketknife that you like, and resolve to keep it for the rest of your life.

8a–b.   **SAFETY GLASSES**

General Description: *A flat plate of hard, clear plastic held in a flexible frame of soft plastic with an elastic strap connected at two points.* The flexible plastic frame is normally translucent and may have ventilation holes. Most safety glasses are large enough to enclose regular eyeglasses.

Habitat: Found near machinery and hazardous liquids. Sold by hardware stores and home centers. Distinguish them from swimming goggles, which neither fit over regular glasses nor are shatterproof.

Primary Use: Shielding the eyes from injury from splashing fluids and flying debris that result from using tools and machines. Ordinary hammering on another tool or on any piece of metal is liable to throw debris, and is not safe without eye protection.

Operating Principle:	Photons pass easily through transparent plastic while flying debris hits the plastic and bounces off.
Variations:	Prescription eyeglasses can be worn as safety glasses if made of shatterproof plastic and equipped with side shields; note, however, that eyeglasses are no help against splashed fluids. Some people prefer a full-face safety shield on an adjustable headband. In the absence of safety glasses, you could do worse than wearing ski goggles.

How to Use: **1. Choose safety glasses that fit your face (and over your eyeglasses, if needed) as well as the job.**

2. Before beginning work that might throw fluids or debris into the air, put safety glasses on. Adjust them for comfort and make sure they'll stay put while your hands and attention are directed elsewhere.

3. When you are done, remove the safety glasses, wash them, and put them away for next time.

Note: **If your safety glasses fog up, try a full-face shield.**

Tool-Kit Minimum: One pair of safety glasses that fit and are comfortable enough to be worn even when you don't think they're strictly necessary.

9.   **WORK BOOTS**

General
Description:

Heavy leather lace-up footwear, usually tan colored, ankle high, and with deep tread on the soles. Like other shoes, work boots cover your feet. Unlike high heels, these are designed to prevent pain in your toes.

Habitat:

Garage, workshop, and coat closet. Sold by shoe stores. Distinguish from hiking boots and ski boots by their tan or yellow color, flat sole, and deep tread.

Primary
Uses:

Protecting the handyperson from falls on slippery surfaces. Protecting the handyperson's feet from injury due to dropped tools or cutting tools that go awry.

   If you can't keep your footing, you can't effectively use a tool. Many activities calling for tools (for example, digging holes with a foot-propelled spade) directly involve the operator's feet. Many others (moving lumber, carving wood) put the feet at risk of injury. Comfortable work boots are essential safety gear.

Secondary
Uses:

Protecting the project from skid marks: Tan work boots with light-colored tread will not leave black traces on newly installed hardwood floors.

Variations:

Some work boots have steeltoe caps inside, best when working with a chain saw or portable circular saw. In the absence of work boots, choose motorcycle boots or Doc Martens, or even sneakers, but not sandals.

How to Use:	1.	**Choose work boots that fit and that are appropriately armored for the task.**
	2.	**Put on a pair of socks. Put on and lace up the work boots.**
Note:		**Snow-melting salt rots leather boots. Begin the snow season by rubbing mink oil into the leather, and wash the boots in the spring.**
Tool-Kit Minimum:		One pair of tan leather steel-toed work boots.

II. Cleaning and Maintenance

Every tool-using (and mess-making) project goes better when you have removed the distractions of dirt and old or broken parts. Every installation includes preliminary clean-up before you can begin, plus final clean-up after you're done. Your tranquility, and that of the people you live with, depends on diligent and cheerful clean-up before, during, and after household projects.

10. **BENCH BRUSH**

General Description:
: *A dense fringe of soft, finger-length bristles sprouting from a wooden or plastic handle.* People differ on whether to clean the work area during the job and immediately afterward or to leave the mess for later on, before the next project can begin. Either way, true karmic progress accrues to handypersons who don't leave messes for others to clean up.

Habitat:
: Workbench tool tray and janitorial closet. Sold in hardware stores and home centers. Distinguish the bench brush from scrubbing brushes by its longer handle and softer bristles.

Primary Use:
: Sweeping debris off the workbench, stepladder, or job site and into the trash can.

Secondary Uses:	Sweeping crumbs off the tablecloth. Cleaning the hearth. When playing charades, represents a sword or a ridiculously large moustache.
Variations:	Small whisk brooms have longer bristles. Cordless miniature vacuum cleaners do similar work.

How to Use: **1.** **Put away tools, fasteners, and parts, and anything else you intend to keep.**

2. **Grasp the brush handle, keeping your wrist at a comfortable angle. Use the bristles to sweep the debris (also called "chips," "scrap," or "swarf") into a heap. For efficiency, sweep with the length of the brush. For a deeper scrub, push the brush endwise.**

3. **Brush the debris directly into a trash can or into a dustpan.**

11.   **BUCKET**

General Description:	*Metal or plastic cup that's bigger than your head but smaller than your torso; more precisely, a container large enough to hold between 1 and 5 gallons (3.8–19 l) of fluid.* A bail, a stiff wire formed into a semicircular shape, is fastened to the rim of the bucket to serve as a handle. High-quality buckets may have a spout plus a small wood or plastic handle centered on the bail.

Habitat: In the broom closet or under the utility sink. Sold by hardware stores, paint stores, and supermarkets. The similarly sized gas can is a hollow container but is enclosed and has two small capped openings.

Primary Uses: Containing, transporting, and dumping water, solutions of cleaning compounds, and other nonvolatile liquids. Catching fluids that drip from leaky plumbing or roofs. Collecting liquid and solid debris generated during messy jobs in tight spaces. Not to be used for gasoline, paint thinner, and other volatile fluids.

Secondary Uses: Transporting live lobsters. Dumping water abruptly (or mischievously) on a car, dog, or person. Can be inverted and stood upon to gain additional height; drywall technicians create stilts by taping sneakers onto empty 5-gallon (19 l) joint compound buckets. In social emergencies a clean bucket can be pressed into service for ice (cover with aluminum foil) or for flowers (cover with gift wrap).

Operating Principle: Gravity. Fluids run downhill to the lowest point, and liquids take the shape of their container.

Variations: Buckets used as commercial containers have lids, some of which fit over the rim (e.g., roofing tar), while others fit inside shaped lips (e.g., paint). Large buckets equipped for cleaning floors may have wheels and a built-in mop-squeezing apparatus.

How to Use:

1. **Choose a bucket larger than the volume of material you intend to put in it.**

2. **Position the bucket where you can fill it, or where the unwanted fluid is landing. Make sure the bucket firmly sits level.**

3. **Fill the bucket (or in the case of descending fluids, allow it to fill) to within a hand's width of the rim.**

4. **Lift the bail to transport the full bucket.**

5. **To empty the bucket, lift the bail with one hand and grasp the near side of the bucket bottom with the other. Tilt the bucket so that its contents spill over the rim, away from you.**

Tool-Kit Minimum:

One 2-gallon (7.5 l) plastic bucket.

12. **FUNNEL**

General Description:

A hollow plastic or metal cone with a large opening (mouth) on one end and a small, finger-sized opening (spout) on the other. The space between the funnel's spout and mouth is called its "neck." The funnel's mouth may be fist-sized to about head-sized; indeed, inverted funnels have been worn as hats in such

movies and television shows as *The Wizard of Oz* and
Star Trek.

Habitat: Under the kitchen or utility sink; in the garage or
            basement among containers of gasoline, kerosene, and
            other fluids. Sold in hardware stores, home centers,
            supermarkets, and auto-parts stores.

Primary   Temporarily enlarging an opening so that fluids may
Use: be transferred into it without spilling; for example,
            filling the table ewer of extra-virgin olive oil. Not for
            solids; granular materials, such as flour or dry sand,
            tend to clog the funnel's neck, though you can poke
            them through with a meat skewer.

Variations: Funnels for reaching deep inside car engines have
            long, flexible spouts. Some funnels have a permanent
            or replaceable filter built into the neck. To separate a
            fluid from solids floating within it, pour through a fil-
            tered funnel, and keep whichever portion you desire.

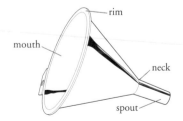

How to Use: 1.   **Match funnel size to container opening and volume of fluid.**

2.   **Place the funnel's spout into the opening and hold the funnel upright, its mouth close to horizontal.**

3.   **Direct fluid into the funnel's open mouth.**

4.   **Listen to the gurgle, whose pitch rises slowly as the container fills, then rises sharply just before it overflows. Stop pouring before it overflows.**

Tool-Kit
Minimum: One funnel for each class of fluids—that is, don't pour gasoline through the same funnel you use for soy sauce, olive oil, or wine.

13.   📷   **ICE BREAKER**

General
Description: *A flat, heavy, metal blade mounted in line with a substantial wooden handle.* The ice breaker's flat iron blade is about the size of your foot, while the smooth metal or wooden handle is almost as tall as you are.

Habitat: Garage or tradesman's truck. Sold by hardware stores and home centers. The in-line blade and handle distinguish the ice breaker from spades and hoes.

Primary Use:	Breaking ice and scraping it off sidewalks, steps, and driveways.
Secondary Uses:	Helpful alongside the pick and spade when digging holes.
Operating Principle:	The heavy wedge.
Variations:	Roofers and tilers use a similar tool, called a mutt, to lift and remove old shingles and tile.

How to Use: 1. **Stand near the ice, though preferably not on it. Hold the ice scraper vertically by its wooden handle, heavy blade pointing down.**

2. **Lift the scraper vertically to knee height and drop it into the ice, causing a fracture. If that fails, pack more energy into the blow by lifting higher. Don't hurl the scraper downward; it won't help, and you might hit your foot.**

3. **Shove the blade under the broken ice and lever up to lift and break.**

14.   **SCRUB BRUSH**

General
Description: *A flat wooden or plastic handle about the same size and shape as your foot with stiff, coarse bristles covering one side.* The bristles of a scrub brush, usually set in round tufts, are about as long as two finger joints.

Habitat: Utility sink and broom closet. Sold by grocery stores.

Primary
Use: Breaking up crud stuck to the workpiece.

Variations: Long-handled scrub brushes extend your reach at the expense of direct pressure over the bristles. Stubby brushes with a rounded clump of bristles clean tires and wheel wells.

How to Use: 1.   **Protect your hands with rubber gloves.**

2.   **Mix detergent into a bucket that is half full of warm water.**

3.   **Soak the brush in the detergent solution and slosh some of the liquid onto the crud.**

4.   **Plant the bristles firmly in the crud and move the brush back and forth. Press as hard as necessary to break up the crud. Continue scrubbing and adding water as needed until all the crud breaks up.**

5. **With a large sponge, wipe away the dirt, rinse with clean water, and wipe again.**

Tool-Kit
Minimum:
One hefty scrub brush with plastic bristles.

15.   **SHOP VACUUM**

General
Description:
A cylindrical tank on wheels, about knee-high, with two fist-sized openings (called "ducts") and an electrical switch, used to clean up dirt and debris. Corrugated plastic hoses plug into each of the openings; the hoses terminate in a variety of specialized, interchangeable attachments. Upon close inspection you'll discover an electrical cord plus latches that connect the tank's top to its hollow body. When the machine is turned on, one of the openings sucks in air continuously while the other expels air.

Habitat:
Garage, basement, and home workshop. Sold by hardware stores and home centers. Closely resembles the *Star Wars* movie robot R2-D2. Though a carpet steamer looks similar, it has a longer, thinner hose and no blow-hole.

Primary
Use:
Capturing mess and debris caused by home renovation projects. Along with air, the inhaling duct sucks the mess into the open end of the hose, transferring it

to the interior of the tank. Match hose attachment to the size and accessibility of the debris.

Secondary
Uses:

Sucking up water and other liquids. Drawing glue into crevices. With the corrugated hose connected to the exhaling duct, the shop vacuum can double as a leaf blower, though not as well as a tool designed specifically for this purpose (see page 92).

Operating
Principle:

Bernoulli principle, whereby the velocity of air being drawn through a duct increases as the duct narrows. The high-speed electric motor spins a fan inside the housing. The fan draws outside air in through one of the machine's two ducts and out through the other, carrying debris along with it. A replaceable internal filter blocks the debris so it drops into the tank.

Variations:

Comes in a variety of sizes. Ordinary household vacuum cleaners do not have the large capacity of the shop vac, nor the ability to manage liquids.

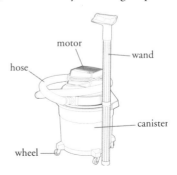

How to Use: 1.   **Choose and connect a hose attachment that matches the mess.**

2.   **Move the unit close to the mess and connect the electrical cord.**

3.   **Switch the electricity on and aim the open end of the hose at one edge of the mess. It will disappear into the attachment.**

4.   **Sweep the attachment from side to side, slowly advancing into the mess. Continue until the mess has all disappeared.**

5.   **Switch off the power, then open the lid to expose the mess, now collected into the tank. Empty the tank into a trash receptacle.**

Tool-Kit   Every home needs one mid-sized shop vac.
Minimum:

16.   **SQUEEGEE**

General   *A T-shaped apparatus with a handle set perpendicular to*
Description: *a metal bracket with a rubber strip.* A close look might
reveal that the bracket retains not one but a pair of
flexible strips, usually made of black or orange rubber,
protruding about a finger's width from the metal. The

wider of these is the squeegee's blade, while the narrower is a backer or stiffener. Squeegees range in length from a hand span to the length of your forearm. They are sometimes found with a person-high wooden handle socketed into the metal one.

Habitat:

Broom closet, utility sink, trunk of cleaning person's car, art supplies cabinet, or even a shower stall. Look for the characteristic T shape with the flexible blade protruding uniformly across the bar.

Primary Use:

Wiping liquid, along with any soluble or floating debris, off smooth glass, plastic, or metal surfaces. The process of wetting window glass with a water solution of cleaning compounds, notably ammonia or vinegar, and then squeegeeing the fluid off, is known as "window washing." It's generally regarded as tedious work: The assertion "I don't do windows" has nothing to do with preference in computer operating systems.

Secondary Uses:

Pushes printing ink through the tightly stretched fabric mesh of a silk-screen frame to transfer an image onto paper or a cotton T-shirt.

How to Use: **1. Choose a squeegee whose blade is no wider than the glass you wish to clean, with a handle long enough to reach the entire surface.**

2.   Wet the surface with a solution of water and ammonia or vinegar, and scrub with a stiff brush to dissolve the dirt and debris.

3.   Orient the squeegee so the stiffener is away from the surface. Starting at the top, press the squeegee's blade tight against the surface. Draw the squeegee down, pulling the liquid and debris ahead of the blade.

4.   If the squeegee does not cleanly remove the water and dirt, vary the angle between the blade and the glass, as well as the pressure.

5.   Wipe the squeegee blade with a damp cloth. Reposition it at the top of the surface where it's still wet and dirty, and repeat.

III. Home Decorating

Home decorating involves changing the color or surface texture of walls, floors, ceilings, and other objects. You're working with such materials as paint, wallpaper, tile, and fabric. Preparing the job site and the workpiece involves making it clean and smooth, so you can then embellish it with decorative materials.

17a–b. **DRYWALL KNIFE**

General Description: *A wood or plastic handle with a thin and flexible metal blade.* A member of the trowel family, drywall knives resemble short-handled kitchen spatulas. The blade is about the length of a finger while its width may range from about two fingers up to the span of a fully spread hand. Confusingly, many drywall technicians apply the same name to the drywall saw (page 38) they use for cutting holes, perhaps because it looks like a regular kitchen knife.

Habitat: Generally stored among painting tools and adjacent to buckets of joint compound (a white or gray mud with the consistency of yogurt), spackle (white mud with the consistency of peanut butter), and rolls of paper drywall tape. Drywall knives are sometimes found encrusted with dried joint compound, and with that, rust.

Primary Uses:	Applying and smoothing joint compound on interior walls made of plaster or drywall (aka sheetrock, gypsum board, or gyprock) in order to fill seams and holes and create neat corners. These procedures are necessary finishing steps when installing new walls and are the best way to repair old walls before repainting.
Secondary Uses:	Removing wallpaper. Spreading wood filler on unfinished hardwood floors, as a step in sanding and finishing. In social emergencies, wide drywall knives can work alongside spatulas when lifting spilled molasses, or when barbecuing for a crowd.
Operating Principle:	Plastic materials (such as drywall compound) take the shape of any harder materials (such as knife blades) that are pressed against them.
Variations:	Some drywall knives have a 90-degree bend, with the vertex in line with the handle, for finishing inside corners. Disposable plastic ones are too wimpy for anything more than a quick spot repair.
How to Use: 1.	**Choose a drywall knife that is wider than the wall defects you wish to fill.**
2.	**Grasp the knife by its handle and use its blade to lift joint compound from the bucket so you can slather it into the wall defect.**

3. Exert medium pressure as you pull the knife across the slathered joint compound. A little experimentation will show you how tilt affects smoothness.

4. Reposition the knife and repeat until you have completely buttered the defect with joint compound and extended the patch a hand span beyond. Make it smooth and neat.

5. Bridge seams by embedding drywall tape in wet joint compound. Fill big holes with new pieces of drywall and joint compound.

6. Use the knife to scrape up excess compound and discard it. It's no saving to return the surplus to the bucket—it's already begun to harden and will only form troublesome lumps.

7. Wait until the compound has thoroughly dried. See whether it has shrunk below the level of the desired surface, and if so, repeat Steps 1 through 7.

8. Once the compound dries level or higher, sand it smooth and level with the surrounding wall. Then it is ready to prime and paint.

9. Wash the drywall knife.

Tool-Kit Minimum:	Do a little drywall work and before you know it, you'll own a bucket full of knives.

18.   **DRYWALL SAW**

General Description:	*A wooden handle in line with a short, stiff-bladed saw blade that comes to a sharp point.* Also called a "wallboard saw" or a "drywall knife," even though another tool is generally known by the same name (page 35).
Habitat:	Toolbox of builder and home decorator. Sold by hardware stores and home centers. Distinguish it from kitchen knives by its saw teeth.
Primary Use:	Sawing holes in the middle of a piece of drywall for such protrusions as light fixtures and switches, power and communications outlets, fans, and vents.
Secondary Uses:	Cutting large pieces of drywall into smaller ones, though most drywallers would prefer a box cutter or utility knife for this task.
Operating Principle:	Drywall is soft enough to be pierced by the sharp point of the saw, creating holes without preliminary drilling.
How to Use: 1.	**Locate and draw the hole on the drywall. In the case of electrical boxes, you can do this by coloring the**

box edges with lipstick, then pressing the box on the drywall to transfer the box outline.

2. Socket the saw handle in your palm and push the point of the blade completely through the middle of the future hole.

3. The saw cuts when you push it into the drywall. It clears the dust, or swarf, out of its teeth when you withdraw it. For neat results, hold the back of the knife blade square to the surface, not tilted in any direction.

4. Saw toward the edge along a curved path so that the flat of the blade ends up on the layout line. Continue sawing all the way around a curved opening, or straight into the corner of a square one.

5. Turn a square corner by almost withdrawing the saw, then twisting its handle so the point makes the turn, then pushing to continue sawing in the new direction. If that seems likely to make a mess, withdraw the saw and repeat Steps 2 through 4, coming at the corner from the other side.

6. Scrub the drywall saw with water and dish detergent when you are done and let it air-dry; drywall dust has an affinity for water vapor, and a dirty saw is certain to rust.

| Tool-Kit Minimum: | Either a drywall saw or a utility knife; see which works better for you. |

19. GLASS CUTTER

| General Description: | *An oddly shaped steel stylus with a tiny steel wheel at the business end and a pea-sized ball at the other.* Close inspection shows a graduated trio of notches above the tiny wheel and a finger-wide flare in the handle just above the notches. Glass cutters usually have colorful enamel from the ball down to the notches, while the notches themselves and the tiny wheel are bare. |

| Habitat: | Glazier's toolbox or home-decorator's toolbox. The tiny wheel, trio of notches, and little round ball are each characteristic and confirm identification. |

| Primary Use: | Scoring or scratching glass to prepare it for breaking along the scored line. This is necessary when making or repairing windows, when making picture frames, and when making artwork with colored glass. |

| Operating Principle: | Pressure is amplified by being concentrated to a point. Glass, an extremely frozen liquid, depends upon pristine surfaces for its strength. Scratching its surface creates a weakness where applied stress will manifest itself as a fracture; the fracture tends to follow the path of the scratch. |

Cutting flat glass is mysterious business, since what you really do is break it in a controlled way. Adepts prefer to drive the glass cutter freehand, but beginners should use a straight edge. Once you get the knack it's fun to try sweeping curves such as stained-glass artists make. Old-timers may urge you to dip the cutter in oil or kerosene but this only makes a mess without doing any good. It's okay to put the tiniest drop of oil on the tiny wheel's axle.

Variations: Some glass cutters have a tiny industrial diamond in place of the steel wheel.

How to Use: **1. Plywood makes a good glass-cutting surface, which should be flat and smooth but not padded. Place the glass flat on the cutting surface, not overhanging.**

2. Orient the glass so the planned cut extends directly away from your body. Set the straight edge on the glass, half the thickness of the glass cutter away from the line. Use the cutter itself to gauge this offset.

3.   Cradle the glass cutter between the thumb and first two fingers of your dominant hand. Your thumb goes under the flare in its handle, your two fingers go on top, with the shaft and ball between the knuckles. Hold it at a comfortable angle, oriented with its three notches toward the thumb side.

4.   Position the glass cutter against the far end of the straight edge and on the cutting line, just inside the boundary of the glass itself. It is not helpful to roll the cutter over the edge of the glass, and doing so may damage the tool.

5.   Adjust the tilt of the cutter so that the notch immediately behind the tiny wheel is parallel to the surface of the glass.

6.   Take a deep breath and draw the cutter along the straight edge. Do it in a single smooth motion, no stopping and no going back.

7.   Set the cutter aside and pick up the glass. Grasp its edge on either side of the scored line, thumbs on top and fingers below. Rotate your wrists away from each other, cleanly snapping the glass.

Note: Thick plate glass may need some help. Lift the near edge of the scored glass and use the ball end of the cutter to tap the underside of the scratched line. Tap from one edge all the way to the other. You might be able to see the fault propagating through the thickness of the glass as you tap. Beginners may find tapping helpful when cutting ordinary window glass, though usually it is not necessary.

Tool-Kit
Minimum:
Knowing how to cut glass identifies you as an adept, and owning a cutter is your badge of office.

20.   **GROUT SAW**

General
Description:
A rigid plastic handle terminating in a short, flat, stiff metal blade. The blade of a grout saw features coarse, hard abrasive granules fused onto its edge.

Habitat:
Tile-setter's toolbox or home decorator's toolbox. Sold by hardware stores, tile stores, and home centers. Distinguish the grout saw by its short blade—about as long as the last joint of your middle finger—and by the coarse spatter of abrasive fused onto its edge, which cannot be thicker than the space between tiles.

Primary
Use:
Raking failed grout out from between ceramic tiles in order to replace it. The space between tiles is filled with a hard material called "grout." Grout is what makes a tiled shower waterproof. Grout is softer than tile so it's liable to deteriorate first, admitting water that soon will destroy the entire installation.

Variations: A rod saw for ceramic tile uses a wirelike blade that is
              coated all around with the same fused abrasive.

How to Use: 1. **Choose a grout saw whose blade is thinner than the
                  spaces between your tiles.**

             2. **Fit the saw's handle into your palm, with your thumb
                  pressed on the flat above its blade.**

             3. **Start at the top of the tile installation and work
                  toward the bottom. Rake the grout saw through the
                  failing grout to break it up and remove it.**

Tool-Kit   Though grout saws are inexpensive, you don't need
Minimum: one until water gets behind the tile.

21.   **HOLE PUNCH**

General   *A pliers-like tool with an asterisk-shaped wheel mounted
Description: on one jaw and a small, perforated anvil mounted on
              the other.* The four or six points of the asterisk actually
              are different-sized hollow tubes with sharp ends, and
              although the wheel does lock in place, it can be
              unlocked and rotated to bring different-sized tubes
              into the operating position. Squeezing the handles
              drives one of the hollow tubes into the anvil, piercing
              a small, round hole through whatever heavy materials
              you place over the anvil (leather is the most com-

mon). A spring in the handles reopens the jaws for
the next hole.

Habitat:

Tool kit of leather worker, upholsterer, or sailmaker.
The star-shaped wheel and pliers-like handles are
characteristic; do not be confused by a grommet set-
ter, a similar tool whose star wheel sprouts short,
thick rods with solid ends.

Primary
Use:

Punching holes in leather and other tough materials,
for example to keep a belt in service after dieting.

Secondary
Uses:

Punched dots of leather or Naugahyde can be glued
on the bottom of craggy lamps and vases so they
won't scratch your grandmother's antique table.

Operating
Principle:

The lever (in the arrangement of handles and pivot)
and the wedge (in the sharp end of the cutters).

Variations:

Individual leather punches, which resemble stubby
pencils, may be purchased in sets of four or six. These
punches have the same sharp, hollow end, plus a slot
in the shank's side that allows the cut piece to come
out. Drive individual punches with a hammer using a
block of wood as an anvil.

How to Use: 1.

**Adjust the hole punch to bring the size you want into
operating position and lock it.**

2. **Mark the locations of the future holes.**

3. **Place the material between the punch and anvil, and wiggle the center of a hole mark into the center of the anvil.**

4. **Squeeze the handles together until the punch passes completely through the material.**

5. **Open the jaws and remove the cutout, or be sure it is entirely within the hollow cutter so that it can't interfere with the next punch.**

Tool-Kit Minimum:
This tool looks so weird and complex that you'll want to own one even if you never need to use it.

22. 📷   **MASTIC TROWEL**

General Description:
A flat plate of thin metal about the size of your foot with notched edges and a centered handle; used for spreading controlled amounts of glue, tile cement, and other thick materials. The mastic trowel is a traditional mason's tool adapted to contemporary materials and techniques. Usually there is a different notch pattern on each edge, with no notches on one short edge.

Habitat:
Tile-setter's toolbox. Sold by paint stores, tile stores, and home centers.

Primary Use:	Raking a glob of adhesive into a uniform pattern of closely spaced beads. The glues or mastics used to set vinyl and ceramic tile must be consistently spread. Too much mastic makes a wasteful mess, but too little jeopardizes the job.
Secondary Uses:	When icing a cake, a new and clean mastic trowel can create beautiful patterns.
Variations:	Disposable mastic trowels, made of plastic, typically resemble drywall knives (page 35).

How to Use:

1. **Choose a trowel whose notch pattern agrees with the adhesive instructions.**

2. **Grasp the handle and use the notched edge to lift a glob from its container. Drop the glob on the surface.**

3. **Shift your grip so the notched edge meets the surface at a 45-degree angle.**

4. **Use the notched edge of the trowel to drag the adhesive across the surface. Sweep the trowel from the shoulder, making a curved pattern. Changing the angle changes the thickness of the spread. With most adhesives there is no harm in working back over an area. Spread only as much surface as you can tile before the adhesive begins to dry.**

5.   Use the unnotched edge to pick up excess adhesive and scrape them into the trash.

6.   Press the tiles into place.

7.   When done, wipe the adhesive off the trowel and wash it with soap and water.

23a–c. 📷   **PAINT CAN OPENER**

General
Description: *A small bent piece of metal.* Conveniently, the shape of an opener is just right for prying lids off paint cans.

Habitat: Home-decorator's toolbox. Sold in paint stores.

Primary
Use: Opening resealable cans of paint, varnish, mastic, and other home-decorating compounds. An opener works on plastic buckets whose lids fit over the rim rather than inside it like metal cans. In the absence of an opener one may be tempted to use a large screwdriver, but being the wrong shape, it's liable to bend the lid and prevent it from resealing.

Secondary
Uses: Most paint can openers will make short work of the caps on beer and soda bottles.

How to Use: 1.   **Spread old newspaper on your worktable.**

2. **Fit the tip of the opener into the groove between lid and can.**

3. **Press down on the end of the opener while keeping a tight grip on the can with your other hand. The lid should begin to lift.**

4. **Move the opener to a new location about a quarter of the way around the rim of the can, reset it, and press down again.**

Tool-Kit
Minimum:
One is essential when working with paint.

 24a–c.

PAINT PAD

General
Description:
A flat plastic holder carpeted with short bristles on one side with a plastic handle on the other side. The paint pad is an alternative to the paintbrush.

Habitat:
Home-decorator's toolbox. Sold by paint stores, hardware stores, and home centers. Distinguish it from the paintbrush by the short bristles (no longer than a fingernail and usually shorter). Most paint pads are red or yellow plastic and have white or yellow bristles.

Primary
Use:
Spreading paint or varnish on floors, ceilings, flat walls, and flat trim. Paint pads require less skill and

attention than paint brushes; they are also less versatile and less efficient, and they don't work on nonflat
moldings or complex objects, such as chairs.

Operating
Principle:
Surface tension in the paint helps it stay on the pad
while you transfer from container to wall. Short, flexible bristles conform to small irregularities in the wall
surface, spreading the paint uniformly.

Variations:
Pads range in size from the width of two fingers up to
the width of a spread hand. Some models have small
plastic wheels on their edges for painting a straight
line up to a corner or molding. Right-angle pads can
paint into the corner between adjacent walls.

How to Use: 1. **Match pad size to job size.**

2. **Spread protective drop cloths or paper, open the
paint can, and pour a small amount into a shallow,
flat-bottomed pan that's larger than the paint pad.**

3. **Dip the pad's bristles into the paint. Do not allow
paint to flow onto the plastic. If the pad has rollers,
wipe them clean.**

4. **Press the loaded pad against the wall and move it to
spread the paint. Begin at the highest point and work
down, working from wet paint onto unpainted walls.**

Note: **Paint pads can be preserved wet for reuse within a day or two by sealing them inside a freezer bag and placing the bag in the fridge. They can be cleaned but cleaning them is so tedious that most painters consider paint pads disposable.**

25. 📷   **PAINT ROLLER**

General Description: *A bent armature or frame made of thick wire that has a handle on one end and a cylindrical roller cover made of nappy fabric or foam rubber mounted on the other end.* The roller frame is about as long as your forearm, while the roller cover itself is about as long as your foot and as thick as your wrist.

Habitat: Home-decorator's toolbox, utility closet, and under the sink. Usually found in or next to a roller pan, which resembles a cake pan but whose bottom slopes to a small, flat well. Sold by home centers, hardware stores, and paint stores.

Primary Use: Transferring and spreading paint on walls, ceilings, and floors. Rollers are more efficient than either brushes or pads for painting flat walls and ceilings. However, because a roller cannot paint a clean edge, it is always used with a paint pad or brush. The roller cover is disposable and replaceable; the wire armature and handle, called the roller frame, should be reused.

Operating
Principle: Surface tension in the paint helps it stay on the roller.
             The roller nap conforms to irregularities in the wall
             surface, spreading the paint uniformly.

Variations: Roller covers come with different lengths of nap for
             painting textured surfaces; they're also available in
             patterned foam for creating decorative effects. Trim
             rollers, as wide as your hand, are for baseboards and
             trim. Double-wide rollers can speed the painting of
             long hallways and cathedral ceilings. Mini rollers,
             which are about the size of a hot dog and which hold
             a surprising amount of paint, are very effective inside
             closets and cupboards, on moldings and trim, and on
             clapboard siding where they can paint the face and
             the adjacent edge at once. Most roller frames can be
             equipped with an extension handle.

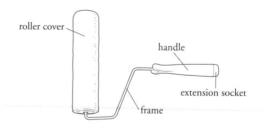

roller cover

handle

extension socket

frame

How to Use: 1. **Since rollers cannot paint a clean edge, prepare for
                 rolling by using a paintbrush to outline the zone to
                 be painted.**

2. Choose a roller whose nap corresponds to the surface: short for flat and smooth, long for rough and irregular. If at the end of the job you intend to clean the roller for reuse, prepare now by dampening the nap with the same solvent that dissolves the paint (water for latex paint, mineral spirits for oil).

3. Pour paint from its bucket into a roller pan. Dip the roller in the paint, then distribute it evenly by rolling on the sloped bottom of the pan.

4. Lift the roller and paint a large W. Roll back and forth across the W to spread the paint into a uniform coating. If the paint spatters, you're rolling too fast.

5. Reload the roller and repeat, working from wet paint into unpainted areas.

6. When finished, slide the roller cover off the roller frame. It can be preserved for a day or two by sealing it inside a plastic bag and placing it in the fridge. Roller covers are inexpensive and difficult to clean, so most painters consider them disposable.

26a–c.

PAINTBRUSH

General Description: *A comfortable handle sprouting a dense, in-line cluster of finger-length bristles.* Paintbrushes are used to transfer liquid paint from its container to the workpiece. They also spread the paint into a thin and uniform coating and smooth its surface before drying.

Habitat:
Home-decorator's toolbox, utility closet, and under the sink. Sold by home centers, hardware stores, and paint stores. Do not be confused by the bench brush or by the scrub brush. Brushes made for paint are distinguished by dense bristles tightly wrapped inside the characteristic metal ferrule, with the bristles and handle aligned.

Primary Use:
Painting. People are in the habit of painting almost everything, including buildings (inside and out), automobiles, furniture and decorative objects, and even their own fingernails.

Secondary Uses:
With clean, new paintbrushes, you can baste meat on the barbecue or brush dust off delicate objects.

Operating Principle:
The huge amount of capillary surface among closely spaced bristles allows them to hold and move paint without excessive dripping.

Variations:
Early paintbrushes had bristles made of plant fiber or animal hair crudely tied around one end of a wooden handle; they were only marginally effective, not unlike early paint. For the last 100 years paintbrushes have employed a wraparound metal ferrule for con-

necting the bristles to the handle. This technology permits making a brush that is both wide and flat, so it can transfer, spread, and smooth the paint with great efficiency. Modern brushes have nylon or polyester bristles, which retain their stiffness better and wear longer than traditional animal-hair bristles. They can be used in every kind of paint.

Paintbrushes are made in an almost infinite variety of widths. Artists favor small animal-hair brushes for creating pictures.

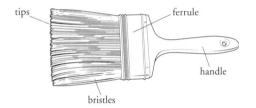

tips   ferrule   handle   bristles

How to Use:

1. **Spread protective drop cloths or newspaper to catch stray paint.**

2. **Choose a brush whose size corresponds to the job. For walls and cutting in corners, choose a brush about as wide as your palm. For small objects such as window casings, choose a brush about as wide as the object itself.**

3. **Prepare the brush by dipping it in the solvent for the paint (water for latex, mineral spirits for oil), then shake it out. This makes the brush easy to clean later.**

4.   Prepare the paint by opening its container and transferring a portion to a disposable container that's wide
enough for the brush.

5.   Grip the ferrule between thumb and fingers; nestle
the handle on the web between thumb and forefinger.

6.   Load the brush by dipping its bristles into the disposable container of paint. Dip to about two-thirds
the bristles' length.

7.   Unload excess paint and prevent drips by tapping the
bristles inside the container. Don't wipe the brush
across the rim, which will unload too much paint.

8.   Deposit and spread the paint on the workpiece by
wiping the bristles across the surface. Begin at the
highest point and work down, working wet paint
onto unpainted areas. Dab into corners and recesses.

9.   Smooth the paint and pick up drips by lightly dragging the bristles across the surface. For best results
drag in one direction only.

10.   To store the brush for a few days without cleaning it,
bundle it tightly in plastic wrap and refrigerate.

11.   To clean the brush, paint it as dry as you can on old
newspaper, then dip it in a small container of the

appropriate solvent and paint it dry again. Wash it in warm water with dishwashing detergent until the water runs clear. Hang the brush by the hole in its handle so the bristles dry straight.

Tool-Kit
Minimum:

For your next big paint job, treat yourself to a professional-quality paintbrush, which will produce nicer results.

27.   **PUTTY KNIFE**

General
Description:

Short, stiff-bladed knife with a square end. The blade is about as long and wide as two fingers. The square end of the blade may have a blunt bevel toward one side.

Habitat:

Toolbox of builder or home decorator. Sold by paint and hardware stores. Don't be confused by similar drywall knives whose blades are thin and flexible.

Primary
Uses:

Pressing and smoothing window putty when installing or replacing glass. Pressing glazier's points (tiny glass-retaining triangles of metal) into the window frame before applying putty.

Secondary
Uses:

Scraping paint and wallpaper. Prying up broken tile. Busting putty off broken windows. In social emergencies, opening clams and spreading cheese.

How to Use: 1.   **Hold the putty knife in your dominant hand with your thumb pressed on the handle nearest the blade, the handle resting on the knuckle of your index finger.**

2.   **Use the putty knife to butter a thin layer of glazing compound (putty) where the glass will rest inside a clean and primed window frame.**

3.   **Set the glass in the bed of putty and press it down. Use the end of the putty knife to push glazier's points flat onto the glass and into the wooden frame, trapping the glass.**

4.   **Use your fingers to roll out a long bead of putty and press it into the corner all around the glass. Make the bead thick enough to cover the glazing points.**

5.   **Starting at a corner, press the putty knife into the glazing compound, with the square end of the blade bearing on the glass and also on the frame. Tilt the handle forward about halfway toward flat. Press hard as you pull the knife along the bead of putty. When you get it right the knife will press the putty tight onto the glass and window frame, leaving a smooth, flat surface and creating a weatherproof seal.**

6.   **Repeat all the way around the frame. Use the tip of the knife to make tidy corners.**

7. **Use the knife like a kitchen spatula to pick up excess glazing compound from the glass and window frame. Return it to the can.**

8. **Clean the knife by wiping with a rag. Remove dried glazing compound with mineral spirits.**

Tool-Kit
Minimum:

A putty knife is a versatile, general-purpose tool that every handyperson should have.

28. **RANDOM ORBIT SANDER**

General
Description:

A handheld power tool whose flat, round base pad accepts replaceable disks of abrasive material and which, when powered up, rapidly rotates the abrasive disk in an interesting rosette pattern. The random orbit sander is bigger than your doubled fists but smaller than your head. It has an on/off electrical switch, as well as a speed-control dial, plus a small cloth sack sticking out from one side. When you turn the electrical switch on, the machine makes a whirring sound and the sanding disk vibrates. Dialing up the speed increases the pitch of the whirring sound. The round base pad has a Velcro-like coating that sticks tight to the matching coating on the back of the abrasive disks. Thus you can exchange abrasive disks by peeling them off the base and pressing a new one in place. The disks have a pattern of holes that corresponds to holes in the sander's pad; these draw the sanding dust into the cloth bag.

The figure, or grain, of wood results from its fibrous nature. All other sanding tools and techniques require close attention to sanding with the direction of the grain and never across it, which would leave deep scratches. The random orbit sander solved that. You can sand right across a joint between two pieces of wood without worrying about cross-grain scratches.

Habitat: Home-decorator's toolbox and woodworking shop. Sold by home centers and hardware stores. Recognize it by its round, Velcro-attached abrasive disks, and finally by its variable speed control. Fine distinctions: Old vibrating sanders are about the same size but have square pads; old orbital sanders are the same size or larger and have round pads, but do not have a variable speed control.

Primary Uses: Smoothing wood, plaster, or metal surfaces before applying such finishes as paint or varnish, and smoothing intermediate coats of paint or varnish as preparation for applying the next coat. By orbiting in a random rosette pattern, the abrasive disk erases its own marks, a feature that revolutionized the sanding of wood.

Secondary Uses: Removing wood, metal, or plastic from an object or part in order to change its shape or refine its edges.

When equipped with a lamb's wool pad, one can polish with car wax or furniture wax.

Operating
Principle:
The pad is fastened to a small, electrically driven planetary gear rotating inside a larger ring gear. This arrangement makes the pad describe a rosette pattern.

Variations:
Detail sanders have triangular pads for getting into tight corners. Some random orbit sanders have adhesive pads, which are not reusable.

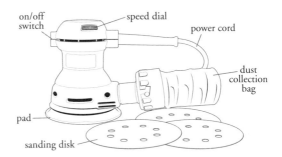

on/off switch — speed dial — power cord — dust collection bag — pad — sanding disk

How to Use: 1.   **With the sander unplugged, remove the old abrasive disk and install a fresh one. Reconnect the electricity.**

2.   **Hold the sander just above the workpiece and switch on the power. Lower the pad gently and evenly onto the surface.**

3.   Slowly move the sander back and forth across the workpiece, being sure to cover all of it without dwelling anywhere. Pressing hard is counterproductive; the sander's own weight plus gentle steering does the job. When you want to stop, lift the sander off the surface before switching the power off.

4.   To assess the smoothness of a sanded surface, look at it under angled light, which reveals defects by their shadows. Lightly stroke the surface with your fingertips, which can sense defects and variations the eye cannot see.

5.   Before changing to a finer abrasive, clean the workpiece with your bench brush (page 22). When sanding between coats of finish, clean the surface with a tack cloth or by vacuuming.

Note: Begin with coarse abrasive and work the entire surface before switching to the next-finer abrasive. Proceed through the available grits without skipping until you achieve the desired degree of smoothness.

Tool-Kit Minimum: Anyone who wishes to refinish furniture will not regret investing in a random orbit sander.

29a–f.   **SCRAPER**

General
Description:
A metal handle with a replaceable razor blade for lifting wallpaper and paint off walls, windows, and trim. Small, hand-sized scrapers take single-edge razor blades; large, arm-sized scrapers use a sharp, replaceable blade about as long as your middle finger. Some scrapers have a safety mechanism for retracting the blade into the handle.

Habitat:
Home-decorator's toolbox. Sold by hardware stores, home centers, and paint stores.

Primary
Uses:
Scraping old wallpaper and peeling or blistered paint off walls and trim, as preparation for applying new wallpaper or paint. Scraping paint off window glass. Failing paint can be removed with chemical strippers, but these powerful mixtures not only are costly but also emit noxious fumes, so they are best reserved for furniture and moldings that are too complex to scrape.

Secondary
Uses:
Scraping ice off the car windshield or sticky labels off products.

Variations:
The hook scraper, which has a replaceable blade shaped like a shallow U with two resharpenable edges, is a heavy tool for raking failed paint off exterior walls. Some hook scrapers have a second, doorknob-style handle for applying muscle right over the blade.

How to Use: 1.   Scraping failed paint and wallpaper makes a glorious mess, so clear the room, lay drop cloths, line your largest trash barrel, and fetch the shop vacuum.

2.   Choose a small scraper for cleaning window glass and a wide one for wallpaper or paint.

3.   Find a spot where the old covering has already begun to lift. Hold the scraper at a low angle to the wall and slide it under the old covering.

4.   Push the scraper under the covering and, if you can, simultaneously pull the loose material off the wall.

Note: Both wallpaper and paint are liable to conceal nasty spots that need repair (see drywall knife, page 35), and to harbor tough places that will not yield and need preparation (see random orbit sander, page 59). Scraping wallpaper and paint is nasty work, and sometimes it's just not possible to complete the job. Just cut away whatever's loose, sand shiny spots to dullness and abrupt discontinuities to shallow slopes, then lay the new stuff right over the old.

30.   **SEAM ROLLER**

General
Description: *A small wooden roller mounted in a metal bracket on the end of a short wooden handle.* The roller is about

the size of your big toe. Its working face is not flat, but slightly crowned, which allows the operator to concentrate the rolling pressure simply by tilting the roller handle.

Habitat:

Home-decorator's toolbox or wallpaper trough. Sold by hardware stores, home centers, and paint and wallpaper stores. The crowned face distinguishes it from the veneer roller, which has a flat face but is otherwise identical.

Primary Uses:

Pressing the seams of freshly pasted wallpaper tight onto the wall. Regluing wallpaper seams.

Secondary Uses:

Pressing freshly glued plastic laminate onto a countertop. Pushing the last bit of toothpaste out of the tube. Flattening a glued seam in fabric when sewing.

Operating Principle:

A roller can be used to exert and distribute pressure without adding any sideways sliding force. A crowned roller can focus the pressure onto a narrow band.

How to Use:

1. **With two wallpaper strips pasted on the wall next to one another, use the wallpaper brush and your fingers to bring the seams tightly together with no overlap.**

2. **Starting at the top of the seam, use the roller to press both adjacent edges tight. If excess wallpaper paste squeezes out, wipe it with a damp sponge.**

31. 📷   **SEWING AWL**

General
Description:

A thick upholstery needle mounted on a wood or plastic handle with a spool of heavy, waxed thread that feeds down a channel cut in the side of the needle and through a hole near its sharp point. There's a compartment inside the handle for spare needles and a little wrench for changing them.

Habitat:

Tool kit of upholsterer, tent mender, leather worker, or sail maker. Sold by leather shops and craft stores. The built-in thread reel and solid needle distinguish the sewing awl from the rug hooker's punch needle, which is thick, hollow, and has no reel.

Primary
Use:

Sewing heavy fabric or leather. Also works on many flexible plastics. This tool is a rudimentary sewing machine, and it forms a stitch the same way a full-size computer-controlled model does.

Operating
Principle:

The thick needle comes to a point (wedge) steep enough to push its way through dense mats of fiber.

Variations:

The sewing awl represents a gamut of ancient tools and ingenious devices for making field or at-sea repairs on leather and fabric. Sailors also know how to sew with rope, which requires fitting the frayed end with a hard and pointy tip called a "fid."

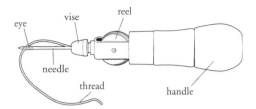

How to Use: 1. **Pin or clamp the materials to be sewn in their final position. Chalk the line to be sewn, called the "seam," on the top layer of material.**

2. **Load the sewing awl with heavy waxed thread whose color matches the material, then bring the free end of the thread down the needle's channel and out through its hole.**

3. **Seat the handle of the sewing awl in the palm of your hand. Brace your index finger just below the top of the needle.**

4. **Starting at one end of the seam, push the point of the needle straight through both layers of material.**

5. **With the needle sticking through the material, pull out enough thread to reach beyond the other end of the seam.**

6. Hold the long thread in your free hand while you pull
    the needle back through the material.

7. Step the point of the needle a stitch-length along the
    seam line and push it straight through again. If the
    needle sticks, wax it.

8. Withdraw the needle partway, which pulls its thread
    into a small loop. Feed the long, free end of thread
    through the loop, then pull the needle back up.
    Tighten the loop on the free thread. This forms the
    first stitch.

9. Repeat to the end of the seam, then feed both threads
    through to the back side of the material, make a tack-
    ing stitch and/or a knot, and cut them close.

---

32.   **STEPLADDER**

General
Description:

*A wood or metal contraption about as wide and tall as
you are that hinges open to form a tall, inverted V shape.*
A close look shows that one side of the V consists of
two upright stanchions or rails separated by flat horizontal slats, or steps, while the other side consists of
two narrow stanchions held apart by a pair of diagonal braces. The top of the stepladder, above its hinge,
is a double-wide step.

Habitat:	Basement and garage. Sold by hardware stores, paint stores, and home centers. Look for the characteristic steps and hinge apparatus.
Primary Use:	Reaching places that are taller than you are by climbing up the ladder's steps, for such purposes as painting, changing lightbulbs, and accessing shelves.
Secondary Uses:	Make a large, sturdy, and temporary worktable by placing a closed stepladder flat across a pair of saw horses, then adding a sheet of plywood on top of that. Make a temporary scaffold by placing heavy planks across corresponding steps of two stepladders.
Operating Principle:	The hinge makes the ladder compact for storage as well as for transporting through doorways, while allowing it to unfold into a wide and stable platform.
Variations:	Some stepladders have multiple hinges with locking mechanisms, permitting them to be set in stairwells.

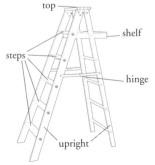

How to Use: 1.   **Choose a ladder that is tall enough for you to reach the job without having to stand any higher than the third rung from the top.**

2.   **Place the ladder directly below the work site.**

3.   **Open the ladder and flip its tool shelf down. If the hinge mechanism includes a locking brace, be sure to lock it, usually by pressing down at its center.**

4.   **Place your tools and materials on the ladder's shelf or in your pockets.**

5.   **Face the ladder and grasp its stanchions. Step on the bottom rung, then the next rung, and so on. However, do not climb so high that you cannot steady yourself by holding onto the top of the ladder itself.**

6.   **Do the work you went up there for, then bring your tools and materials down with you.**

Tool-Kit   One 6-foot (1.8 m) stepladder.
Minimum:

33. 📷   **TILE NIPPER**

General   *A pair of crossed steel handles connected by a pivot pin*
Description: *and ending in short, clawlike jaws that terminate in a*

sharp edge and do not quite meet when fully closed. The small jaw-inserts are made of a material harder than steel, usually tungsten carbide. A stout spring reopens the jaws so the nipper can be operated with one hand (important because the operator must hold the tile to be nipped in the other hand).

Habitat:	Tile setter's toolbox. Sold in hardware stores and home centers. Distinguish from regular pliers and wire cutters by the sharp jaws that do not quite meet.
Primary Uses:	Nipping or nibbling chips off ceramic tile to make it fit around such obstacles as sinks, light switches, and pipes. Also works on heavy plastic.
Operating Principle:	The lever. Nippers have relatively long handles operating their short jaws for large mechanical advantage against the reluctant tile.
Variations:	Some nippers have a built-in scoring wheel for making a scratch on the tile where you intend it to break (see glass cutter, page 40, for instructions on how to do this).
How to Use: 1.	**Put on your eye protection and your work gloves.**
2.	**Hold the ceramic tiles in place so you can draw the line to be cut.**

3.   Use a glass cutter or the scoring wheel on the nippers to scratch the cut line. Scratch hard enough to break the surface of the ceramic glaze.

4.   Hold the tile in one gloved hand, the nipper in the other, and set the tile between the jaws of the nipper. Start near a corner or an edge.

5.   Squeeze the handles so the nipper's jaws close tight on the tile. Squeeze until the tile breaks. Wiggling the tool does not change its leverage and won't help much.

34a–b. 📷   **WALLPAPER BRUSH**

General Description: *A flat wooden handle about the length of your forearm with a coarse, stiff fringe of white or yellow bristles attached all along one of its edges.* The bristles and assembly are shorter than, but as narrow as, your middle finger. Usually the handle has an indentation all along its length, enabling a good grip at any point, even when wet and slippery.

Habitat: Home-decorator's toolbox or wallpaper trough. Sold by paint and wallpaper stores, home centers, and hardware stores. Distinguished from scrub brushes by its length and narrowness, from paintbrushes by its end-to-end bristles and handle shape, and from the bench brush by its thinness and non-extending handle.

Primary Use:	Spreading paste on the back of wallpaper prior to hanging it on the wall. Pressing the pasted paper tightly onto the wall.
Variations:	Some wallpaper brushes have a paintbrush-style handle. Some wallpaper technicians prefer to use a large, coarse sponge for the same task.

How to Use:

1. **Cut a length of wallpaper to the height of the wall plus a hand span.**

2. **Fold the wallpaper loosely back on itself and wet it in the wallpaper trough (page 74).**

3. **Spread the wet wallpaper out flat on the worktable, back side up.**

4. **Use the wallpaper brush to spread wallpaper paste on the back of the paper. Work in a broad sweeping motion. With prepasted paper, skip this step.**

5. **Fold the strip of wallpaper in half, wet pasted side facing pasted side. Fold it again, so that it looks like a large book (which is what it is now called). Let the booked paper sit for 20 minutes so the paste can cook, while you repeat Steps 1 through 5 with new strips.**

6. **Carry the first wallpaper strip to its destination on the wall and unfold one flap of the book. Press its**

pasted side against the top of the wall using the wall-paper brush.

7.   Carefully unfold the booked wallpaper and align it with the wall corner or with the edge of the adjacent strip. Then use the wallpaper brush to press it against the wall and to work any air bubbles out to the edges.

8.   Cut the excess paper off at the floor or baseboard using a fresh single-edge razor blade.

35. 📷   **WALLPAPER TROUGH**

General
Description: *A plastic vessel about as long as your arm and as wide and deep as your spread hand, open all along the top and with a flat, completely closed bottom.* Too floppy to be carried around when full of water, the wallpaper trough must be settled firmly on the floor or work table before you fill it from your bucket.

Habitat: Home-decorator's toolbox, usually stored full of related wallpapering tools such as the wallpaper brush and the seam roller. Sold by paint and wallpaper stores, home centers, and hardware stores. In volume and function the wallpaper trough is similar to the bucket, though quite different in shape.

Primary
Use:

Wetting wallpaper to activate its coating of paste, or to prepare it for being coated with paste.

Secondary
Uses:

Storing partial rolls of wallpaper, which generally are too short to be useful but too long to discard. Protecting extralong hero sandwiches during transport. Lining a window box for planting.

How to Use:

1. **Set the wallpaper trough on the worktable and fill it about halfway with clean water.**

2. **Cut a strip of wallpaper to length and loosely roll it with the patterned side in.**

3. **Dunk the wallpaper in the trough of water and slosh it up and down to be sure it is completely wet. Let it soak for a few minutes.**

4. **Remove the wallpaper for pasting and booking (see wallpaper brush, page 72), and repeat.**

IV. Garden and Yard

Preparing the earth for planting, installing seeds and plants, and tending to them as they grow is heavy and repetitive work, using simple but sophisticated tools that have evolved through thousands of years. Powered equipment has made a dent in the labor, but at a price: You have to own and maintain the machinery.

36.   **BOW SAW**

General
Description: *A C-shaped steel frame about as long as an adult's arm with a thin strip of metal bolted across the open side of the C.* The metal strip of a bow saw, called the "blade," has sharp, toothlike serrations all along one edge. In smaller versions the C-shaped frame is flattened toward a triangular shape.

Habitat: Garage or basement, generally found among gardening and pruning tools. Sold by hardware stores and home centers. The configuration of frame and blade is sufficient for identification.

Primary
Uses: Cutting limbs off trees to promote their health or a more pleasing silhouette, called "limbing." Cutting small trees and brush off level with the ground, called "felling" small trees, and "clearing" brush. Cutting felled trees and limbed branches to firewood length,

called "bucking." Carry a bow saw when hunting for a Christmas tree.

Operating
Principle:

The wedge. Sharp, chisel-like metal teeth, or wedges with extreme taper, will sever wood fibers when pushed into them. Repetition ultimately divides a single length of wood into two lengths. Tension by the frame keeps a thin blade stiff and efficient.

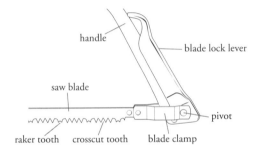

How to Use: 1. **Choose a bow saw that you can comfortably heft one-handed.**

2. **Assess the tree or limb to be cut and visualize the line of the cut. Draw the line with chalk, crayon, or marker.**

3. **Grasp the saw frame with your dominant hand just above the end of the blade and set the blade's teeth on the line of the cut.**

4. **Plant both feet firmly.**

5. **Make sure your other hand, if not on the saw frame, is not near the line of the cut, because the saw could catch and jump, cutting you.**

6. **Push the saw blade and observe the sawdust, or swarf, that it creates. If the blade is sharp, the saw should create swarf under its own weight plus gentle pressure. If it doesn't do this, the blade is dull and needs replacing.**

7. **Pull the full length of the blade back, then continue pushing and pulling until it chews completely through the wood.**

8. **If you are removing a heavy limb, do it in three stages. Make the first cut a hand-span away from the main trunk and saw upward from the bottom of the branch about a third of the way. Make the second cut down toward the bottom cut. This removes the weight of the branch without tearing the tree's bark, but leaves a stub. Remove the stub with a downward cut just beyond the bark collar where the branch emerges from the trunk.**

Tool-Kit   Keep a bow saw for the times when you want to cut
Minimum: wood beyond the reach of extension cords.

37.   **FORK**

General
Description:
A short wooden pole with a D-shaped handle on one end and four flat, gently curved metal blades (called "tines") on the other. The tines of a garden fork are about as long as an adult's forearm, spaced two to three finger-widths apart.

Habitat:
Garden shed or garage. Sold by home and garden centers. Distinguish it from the similar pitchfork by the short D handle and square, blunt tines.

Primary
Uses:
Loosening garden soil as preparation for planting. Breaking up bales of hay or compost before working them into the soil. Moving difficult materials such as wet leaves, manure, or smoldering carpet.

Operating
Principle:
The lever. The garden fork is designed to be driven into the earth by foot power, then rocked back and forth by its handle to lift and loosen the soil.

Variations:
Some gardeners prefer long handles.

How to Use: 1. **Take an easy stance and hold the fork by its handle. Plant the tines of the fork on the soil.**

2. **Lift your dominant foot and place it on top of the armature holding the tines. Push your foot down on the fork, driving its tines into the soil.**

3.   **Lever the handle back and forth to loosen the soil. Lever it down to lift the clump of soil from the planting bed. Turn the fork on edge to drop the clump of soil.**

4.   **Use the edge of the fork like an axe to chop the clump of earth.**

5.   **Working backward across the garden, repeat Steps 1 through 5.**

38.   **GARDEN CART**

General
Description: *A large box on two wheels with acutely leveraged handles.* The spoked wheels of a garden cart are knee-high, mounted one on either side of the box. Made of plywood, plastic, or metal, the three-sided box is large enough for such heavy and awkward loads as bales of hay or peat moss, firewood, compost, sand, and rocks. The location of the axle and of the cart's skid or prop allow the cart to stand level when unattended and make it easy to tilt upward by lifting the handles.

Small, two-wheeled carts are the mainstay of peasant economies worldwide because they allow an unaided person to transport more than his or her own weight by pushing and pulling, which is much easier than lifting and carrying. It's difficult to overstate the usefulness of a sturdy cart.

Habitat:	Garden shed, garage. Sold by home centers and (in kit form) by mail-order specialists.
Primary Use:	Moving materials and tools around the yard.
Secondary Uses:	Hauling almost anything: sheets of plywood, old refrigerators, all the drinks for a party, the luggage for a beach vacation, or a hill of earth or gravel.
Operating Principle:	The wheel (allowing forward motion) and the lever (loading and unloading by tipping the cart).
Variations:	The power wagon is a self-propelled, gasoline-powered, high-capacity garden cart with handlebar controls that include a multispeed gearshift. The extremely maneuverable wheelbarrow, which has a single wheel in front of the box, is not as stable and requires more strength to operate since it must be lifted as well as pushed, but it can contain and transport wet plaster or cement.
How to Use: 1.	**Choose a cart that is big enough for the variety of loads you are likely to encounter, but not so huge you can't push it by yourself.**
2.	**Place the cart adjacent to the load and add the material into the cart. For extremely heavy objects, lift the handles to stand the cart up on its front end. Rock**

the heavy object (use a pry bar, page 159, if necessary) so you can slide the edge of the cart underneath it. Then tilt the cart back to its level position, bringing the heavy object along with it.

3.   Terrain determines whether to push or pull the cart. Conquer slopes by tacking back and forth, gaining (or losing) a comfortable amount of elevation with each traverse.

4.   When you reach the cartload's destination, park the cart level for unloading. Loose loads such as compost or gravel or very heavy objects may be dumped by lifting the handles to stand the cart up on its front end. Manually remove fragile objects from the cart.

5.   Store the garden cart indoors or inverted so the box doesn't fill up with rainwater.

Tool-Kit   Every homestead needs a sturdy cart.
Minimum:

39a–b.   **HEDGE SHEARS**

General   *Two flat metal blades on wooden or plastic handles con-*
Description: *nected at their midpoint by a pivot to form an X.* The metal is bent, or cranked, just before the handles meet the pivot. The two forearm-length blades do not meet

but instead pass over one another, making a character-istic snicking sound. Hedge shears are sharp all along their two passing edges, just as scissors are.

Habitat:
Garden shed and garage. Sold by home and garden centers. Distinguish hedge shears from scissors by their much larger size and straight (not looped) handles. Distinguish them from loppers by their longer blades and from secateurs by longer handles as well.

Primary Uses:
Trimming along the edge of sidewalks and planting beds and around trees. Cutting new growth off such shrubs as box, holly, yew, and privet to maintain their size and form. The geometry of hedge shears suits them to cutting clumps of soft grass and new sprouts.

Secondary Uses:
Topiary, that is, trimming shrubs so they resemble reindeer, giraffes, your initials, or geometric shapes such as spheres, cubes, and cones (watch the movie *Edward Scissorhands* to see a master topiary artist at work).

Operating Principle:
The wedge (sharp blades) and the lever (the pivot is the fulcrum).

Variations:
Some clippers have a serrated blade, better for more woody growth.

How to Use: 1.   **Grasp the handles in your two hands, blades parallel to the ground; the cranked handles provide finger clearance when the blades are tight against the ground.**

2.   **Move your hands apart to open the blades.**

3.   **Position the open blades on either side of the grass to be cut, and move your hands briskly together, closing the blades and severing the vegetation. Repeat as needed.**

4.   **Rinse and wipe the shears before putting them away. A drop of oil on the pivot will keep it working smoothly.**

Tool-Kit Minimum: The hedge shear is the only alternative to a noisy string trimmer (page 114).

40.   **HOE**

General Description:	*A long wooden handle with a bent piece of metal attached to one end, usually with a metal collar called a "ferrule."* A garden hoe resembles a kitchen spatula, only the metal piece is attached to a much longer handle. The hoe is a traditional garden tool for breaking up clods of earth, loosening soil, opening a trough for planting seeds, covering seeds, and culling weeds from among new plants.
Habitat:	Garden shed and garage. Sold by home and garden centers. Usually found alongside the rake and cultivator. Distinguish the hoe from the spade by its smaller blade and right-angle bend; from the cultivator by its solid blade not divided into tines.
Primary Use:	Chopping soil and weeds when planting and maintaining vegetable and flower gardens.
Operating Principle:	The long handle means you can work while standing, which is less tiring than stooping or kneeling.
Variations:	The cultivator is a hoelike tool whose blade has been divided into several narrow blades, or tines. Some cultivators have two or more sets of blades.
How to Use: 1.	**Hold the hoe with one hand near the top end of the handle and the other about halfway along its length.**

2. **Place the blade of the hoe on the soil. With one hand as the fulcrum, raise and lower the other so the hoe chops into the soil.**

3. **Hoe briskly to chop clods of earth. To open a trough for planting seeds, turn the hoe up on its corner and draw it toward you. Push with the hoe blade to cover newly planted seeds.**

4. **When done, scrape off dried clods of earth and rinse the hoe in water.**

Tool-Kit
Minimum: One hoe is necessary for planting seeds and weeding.

---

41.   **HOSE**

General
Description: *A long, flexible, hollow tube of rubber or plastic whose thickness matches your thumb and whose length can be many times your total height, with a metal screw coupling on each end.* The couplings on each end of a hose aren't identical—one is a loose, inside-threaded collar, the other is fixed and threaded on the outside. The couplings on hoses and most other two-ended widgets usually are identified as "male" (the part that goes in) and "female" (the part that receives). The faucet has male threads that fit into the female end of the hose, whose other (male) end fits the female cou-

pling on nozzles, sprinklers, or another hose. Gaskets in each connection, like good humor in relationships, can make even a loose fit watertight.

Hoses are stored in coils, either flat on the ground or hanging on a wall bracket, or wound on a reel mechanism designed to keep them from tangling, which hoses seem to do despite your contrary efforts.

Habitat:	Garden shed, garage, and basement. Sold by home and garden centers.
Primary Use:	Delivering water from a faucet for hydrating plants or for washing objects.
Secondary Uses:	Filling (or emptying) water beds. Siphoning water from a fish tank and replacing it. Putting tremendous pressure on glued subassemblies (wrap the empty hose tightly around the subassembly, then expand it by turning on the water). A hose makes a terrific pre-electronic intercom; a whisper sent into one end emerges hardly diminished at the other.
Operating Principle:	Fluids under pressure (the water in the faucet) flow into all parts of their container (the hose) and spurt out through any opening (the end of the hose).
Variations:	Soaker hoses have many holes for dispersing water along their length. Thick, large hoses are capable of carrying enough water for fire fighting and filling

swimming pools. Hoses as short as your arm are perfect for siphoning gasoline out of cars. Straight, rigid hoses are called "pipes."

How to Use: 1.   **Choose a hose (or hoses) long enough to reach from the faucet to the delivery zone.**

2.   **Connect the female end of the hose to the faucet, uncoil the hose, and extend it along the ground. Make sure it does not double back on itself and kink, which shuts off the flow.**

3.   **If the hose has an adjustable nozzle at its open end, close it. If you intend to use a sprinkler, attach it. Otherwise place the free end of the hose on the ground, pointing toward the delivery zone.**

4.   **Return to the faucet and open it.**

5.   **Return to the open end of the hose, adjust the nozzle or sprinkler, and direct the water.**

6.   **When you are done, shut off the water and recoil the hose.**

Note: **To drain all the water out of a hose, decouple it from the faucet, lift it onto your shoulder, and walk its length, feeding the hose over your shoulder as you go.**

Tool-Kit
Minimum:
One hose is sufficient; you'll find it is much more efficient than a bucket.

42. 📷 **LAWN MOWER**

General
Description:
A large, noisy, gasoline-powered contraption with a wheel on each corner and an upright, U-shaped handle. Modern lawn mowers all have a starting mechanism and two filler caps on the main body of the machine, with control cables and levers on the handle. A flat metal blade about as long and wide as your forearm and hand, sharpened near both ends, is housed beneath the main assembly, near to the ground. The blade is bolted onto a short axle sticking straight down. When the engine is started according to the manufacturer's directions, the contraption produces noise and smoke and the blade whirls around like an airplane propeller.

Habitat:
Garden shed or garage. Sold by home and garden centers. Distinguish the lawn mower from similar machines such as the snow thrower by its flat, low-to-the-ground blade.

Primary
Use:
Cutting grass to a short, uniform length in a ritual known as "mowing the lawn." The mower's engine sweeps the blade in a circle, chopping any grass and weeds in its path.

Secondary Uses:	Chopping fallen leaves into small pieces as an alternative to collecting them with a leaf rake.
Operating Principle:	The internal combustion engine works to turn the sharp blade at high speed. The blade cuts through most everything in its path.
Variations:	Some mowers are self-propelled via a drive belt connecting the engine to the rear wheels. Some have large cloth bags that automatically collect some of the cut grass. Electric mowers are quieter than gasoline, not as powerful, and inoperable beyond the reach of their extension cords. Old-fashioned lawn mowers have no engine, relying instead on a reel-shaped twist of blades powered by gears connected to the machine's wheels. Pushing the machine across the lawn turns the wheels and spins the reel of blades.

How to Use: 1.   **Pick a dry day to mow the lawn and a time when other folks are not trying to sleep.**

2. Check the fluids under the mower's two filler caps, one for gasoline and the other for engine oil, and top off as necessary.

3. Adjust the height of the mower wheels to the height you wish to cut the grass.

4. Put on hearing protectors and safety goggles. Mowing might seem benign, but these noisy machines can kick up furious clouds of sand and gravel along with whatever debris might lurk in the tall grass—a stray piece of wire can be extremely dangerous.

5. Start the mower engine by following the instructions in the owner's manual.

6. Push the mower, or if it is self-propelled, steer it across the grass. For safety be sure you do not push the mower across your own foot, and never reach underneath while it's running. Mow so that you cover the entire area of grass exactly once. Try not to mow any rocks or fallen branches, as they are liable to stall the engine and may also damage the blade.

7. Shut the engine off and lower the handles to the ground, raising the mower housing. Reach underneath it with a flat stick to scrape off any clinging grass before parking the mower in its shed or in your garage.

Note: **At the end of each mowing season, drain the gas tank
and run the engine entirely out of gas. This may
make it easier to start the next time.**

Tool-Kit   While you can get away without trimming the edges
Minimum: of your grass, neighborly outrage falls on those who
decline to mow. If you have grass, you need a mower.

43.   **LEAF BLOWER**

General   *A gasoline-powered engine worn on the operator's back*
Description: *like a knapsack with a stout pipe (or wand) as thick as*
your upper arm extending down to the ground. A handle
and trigger mechanism are mounted near the top of a
leaf blower's wand, with a starter pull, choke control,
and single filler cap (typically requires a 50:1 gas-oil
mixture) mounted on the gas engine. When the
engine is running the machine shoots a powerful and
continuous blast of air through its pipe and also emits
a head-splitting noise.

Habitat: Garden shed or garage. Sold by home and garden
centers and power equipment suppliers. The back-
pack-style gasoline engine is characteristic and unique.

Primary   Blowing fallen leaves into manageable piles, onto
Use: planting beds, into the woods, or over a fence.

Secondary Uses: Clearing light snow off driveways and cars. In dry climates, blasting dust and sand off decks, walks, and driveways; in damp climates, blasting puddles or moss off decks and walks.

Operating Principle: The gasoline engine spins a vaned rotor inside a housing, concentrating a high wind and blasting it out through the wand.

Variations: Some blowers are equipped with a tank for spraying orchard trees with fertilizer and pesticide. Small, electrically powered leaf blowers are light, yet powerful enough to clear a condo patio or apartment balcony.

How to Use: 1. **Put on safety glasses, hearing protectors, and workgloves. For best results, blow leaves on dry, windless afternoons.**

2. **Top off the fuel tank with the appropriate mixture of gasoline and oil (check the owner's manual).**

3. **Start the two-cycle blower engine by following the instructions in the owner's manual, adding curses as needed. Some two-cycle engines are stubborn about starting on the first try.**

4. **Wade into the fallen leaves, starting nearest the house and working outward. Direct the wand to blow the leaves into rows and piles.**

5.   **Use a leaf rake to gather the piles into trash bags or
onto a tarp, which you can haul to the compost heap.**

Tool-Kit
Minimum:

Measure your need for a blower by the size of your
carpet of autumn leaves.

44.   **LEAF RAKE**

General
Description:

*A long wooden handle with a flat, fan-shaped cluster of
tines fastened to one end.* The fan of tines on a leaf rake
is about knee-high when you stand the rake on end.
The tines—there'll be 20 or more—are uniformly
bent at right-angles a thumb-length from their tips.
Before there were leaf blowers, there were rakes, and it
is possible to clear autumn leaves from the largest
suburban yard using nothing but a rake.

Habitat:

Garden shed or garage. Sold by home and garden
centers. The flat fan of tines is unique; in an earlier
time leaf rakes had to be distinguished from rug beat-
ers, which had a shorter handle and straight tines.

Primary
Uses:

Sweeping fallen leaves into rows and piles. Cramming
piles of leaves into plastic trash bags.

Secondary
Uses:

Knocking fallen leaves, or snow, out of shrubs.
Raking up cut grass after mowing.

Operating
Principle:

The fan arrangement allows the tines to flex, so they catch leaves without digging into the soil.

Variations:

Small rakes with ten or fewer tines can pull debris out of planting beds without damaging delicate perennials. While bamboo is nicest, rakes are also made of plastic or wire.

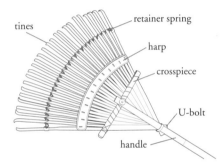

tines — retainer spring — harp — crosspiece — U-bolt — handle

How to Use:

1. **Choose a sunny and windless day. Raking is very difficult when the leaves are heavy with rain or overnight dew. Wear work gloves to prevent blisters.**

2. **Hold the rake with one hand near the top of the handle and the other about halfway down. Take a marching stance with your forward foot on the same side as your upper hand.**

3. **Extend the rake forward into the leaves. Keep the bent tips of the tines close to the ground as you**

sweep the rake alongside your body, bringing leaves along with it.

4.   **Maneuver the leaves into a row, sweep the row into a heap, and push the heap into trash bags or onto a tarp for hauling onto the compost pile or into the woods.**

Tool-Kit
Minimum:
A midsized leaf rake goes with any size garden, and is a quiet alternative to the noisy leaf blower.

45.   **LOPPERS**

General
Description:
Two arm-length handles connected by a pivot or knuckle, with two finger-length blades. Opening and closing the handles also opens and closes the blades, just as pliers and scissors do. One of the blades has a straight, sharp cutting edge, while the other consists of a flat, coppery anvil against which the blade stops.

Habitat:
Garden shed and garage. Sold by home and garden centers. The long handles with short blades are characteristic of loppers.

Primary
Use:
Cutting branches off trees and shrubs. Chopping saplings and branches into manageable lengths.

Secondary
Uses:
Cutting almost any nonmetallic object that will fit into the jaws.

Operating
Principle:

The lever and the wedge. Closing the long handles transmits enormous power to the short, sharp blade.

Variations:

Some loppers have extension handles or geared knuckles for increased cutting power. Bypass loppers have a curved blade and anvil, with the blade passing the anvil instead of landing on it, just as secateurs do.

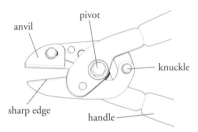

How to Use:

1. **Choose loppers for cutting sticks up to the thickness of your big toe. For thick branches and saplings, choose a pruning saw or bow saw. Wear fabric or leather work gloves.**

2. **Open the loppers and nestle the branch in the jaws.**

3. **Plant your feet firmly for stability, then squeeze the lopper handles together. Enjoy the satisfying crunch as the blade breaks through.**

4. **When cutting overhead, stand a half pace back so the falling branch does not hit you or scratch your face.**

5. **When you're done, wipe the loppers clean. Examine the blade; if it is nicked or dull, repair it with a sharpening stone (page 228) or a fine file (page 283). Put a drop of oil on the knuckle.**

Tool-Kit
Minimum:

Short of a chipping machine, loppers are the quickest way to prune and dismember branches and saplings.

46a–b.   **PICK**

General
Description:

A stout wooden handle, about waist-high when upright, with a heavy, pointed, and somewhat curved iron bit centered on one end, making a T shape. The heavy iron bit of the pick has an open eye in the middle, and the handle flares where it slides through the eye, making a tight fit. The points on the iron bit, each about as long as your foot, are square in cross section.

Habitat:

Garden shed and garage. Sold by home and garden centers.

Primary
Uses:

Breaking up soil and whatever lies below; roughing out gardens, basements, coal mines, graves, and other holes in the ground. Swinging a pick is a whole-body exercise requiring both strength and endurance.

Operating
Principle:

Leverage and momentum: Your shoulder is the axis of rotation and the lever arm is the straight line from shoulder to hand to the far end of the pick's bit. The swing is almost a full circle. The mass being accelerated is the pick's handle plus its heavy iron bit. All this energy explodes when the pick slams into the earth.

Variations: The mattock, whose bit has one pointed end and one flat like an ice breaker or a thick hoe, is better than the pick for chopping through roots.

How to Use: 1.   **Put on work boots and gloves.**

2.   **Take a stable marching stance at a right angle to the future hole.**

3.   **Stand the pick upright, bit on the ground, and grasp its handle with both hands.**

4.   **Visualize where you want the pick to hit. Keep your eye on the target.**

5.   **To gather momentum, make an almost full-circle swing with your arms extended. Swing the pick away from its target as if golfing; momentum will carry it up overhead so you can power the heavy bit down.**

6.   **Lever, don't lift, the pick out of the ground, so it dislodges the rocks and breaks the earth.**

7.   **Repeat until done, clearing debris as necessary.**

47. 📷   **PITCHFORK**

General
Description:

A long wooden handle with a rack of three or more iron tines at one end. The tines are about as long as your forearm and no thicker than your smallest finger, round and smooth, and gently curved toward their sharp-pointed tips. The pitchfork is a robust tool used for digging through compost and mulch and moving material such as straw, hay, or manure, but it is not so tough that you can dig the earth with it.

In the well-known painting *American Gothic,* by Grant Wood, the implement propping up the dour old gent is a pitchfork. Illustrators sometimes depict the Devil holding a three-tine fork that has barbed tips (which identify that tool as a fisher's trident), and sometimes holding a regular three-tine pitchfork (which identifies it as specifically for manure).

Habitat:

Garden shed or horse barn. Sold by farm and garden suppliers. Distinguish the pitchfork from the garden fork by the shape of the tines—these are smooth so hay slides on and off, whereas the garden fork's are thick and sturdy for wrestling with soil.

Primary
Use:

Moving straw and hay for feeding and bedding animals or while gardening. Turning compost.

How to Use: 1.   **Hold the pitchfork in both hands, one near the end of its handle and the other about halfway to the tines.**

2. Take a comfortable marching stance near the hay or straw you intend to move.

3. Break up the bale by poking it with the tines.

4. Pick up a clump of hay on the tines.

5. With one hand as the lever arm and the other as the fulcrum, lift and toss the hay. Station yourself where the pitchfork best extends your reach, getting the job done without a lot of walking back and forth.

Note: Be sure to stand the pitchfork against a wall (tines down) or hang it on a wall (tines up). If you leave it on the ground, people will be at risk of stepping on it.

48. 📷 **RAKE**

General Description: *A T-shaped tool consisting of a long wooden handle with a wide rack of short metal tines attached at one end.* The rake's rack is at a right angle to the handle; its finger-length tines are at a right angle to the rack. All this right angularity is what makes a fallen rake dangerous: step on it wrong, and you risk injury to your foot or levering the handle upward until it hits you.

Habitat: Garden shed or garage. Sold by home and garden centers. Distinguish the garden rake from the leaf rake by its short, rigid tines emerging from a solid bar, versus the leaf rake's flexible fan of long tines.

Primary Use: Smoothing and leveling newly cultivated soil before planting.

Secondary Uses: Breaking up clods of earth while gardening. Combing rocks out of prepared beds of soil and cat droppings out of children's sandboxes. Fishing kites out of trees. Combing the sand in a Zen garden and the long-jump pit at a track meet.

Operating Principle: Rocks and sticks cannot sneak between the rake's tines; they're dragged along with it.

Variations: Small hand rakes with short racks of three tines are for cultivating planted beds and box planters.

How to Use: 1. **Hold the rake with both hands and take a comfortable marching stance.**

2. **Place the tines on the soil. Push and pull the handle so the tines move to and fro.**

3. **To level the surface of the soil, extend the rake far out in front of you and draw it toward you. To cover newly planted seeds, push with the back of the rack of tines. Rake briskly to chop clods of earth.**

4.   **When done, scrape off dried clods of earth and rinse the rake in water.**

Tool-Kit
Minimum: Planting grass, vegetables, or flowers requires a garden rake.

49. 📷   **SECATEURS**

General
Description: *Two hand-sized, plastic-covered metal handles crossed at a pivot, one ending in a sharp, curved blade and the other in an oppositely curved bypass anvil, or "bill."* A spring pushes the handles apart so their normal in-use position is open. A lock mechanism keeps the jaws safely closed when the secateurs (also called "hand-pruners" or "bypass pruners") are not in use. The curved blade passes by the anvil, sliding against it without banging into it.

Habitat: Garden shed or garage. Sold by home and garden centers. Distinguish from pliers by the sharp blade; from loppers by size; and from snips by the bypass anvil.

Primary
Use: Cleanly cutting green stems and new growth off plants, shrubs, and trees.

Secondary
Uses: Cutting flower stems to extend their life. Shaping bonsai trees.

Operating   The curved blade and bypass action make a clean slice
Principle: that does not bruise living plants. This configuration
                also allows cutting a twig right next to the main stem,
                leaving no stump to rot. Where anvil loppers are tools
                of force, secateurs are delicate and precise.

Variations: Anvil pruners are the same size but have a straight
                blade that closes onto a flat anvil, same as long-han-
                dled loppers. Japanese flower snips have bypass blades
                with looping handles.

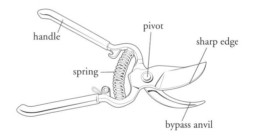

How to Use: 1. **Choose secateurs when you want to make a clean cut
                in green stems.**

             2. **Hold the secateurs in one hand. Use the anvil to
                catch the stem you want to cut, sliding it close to the
                pivot.**

             3. **Squeeze the two handles together so the sharp blade
                slices through the stem.**

4. **Rinse the secateurs in running water when done. Inspect the blade for damage and touch it up with a sharpening stone or fine file (page 283).**

50. **SNOW SHOVEL**

General
Description:

A wide tray or blade of sheet metal or tough plastic mounted on one end of a stout wooden shaft with a D handle on the other. The blade is bent to form short sides nearest the handle, but it's entirely open and flat at the working end.

Habitat:

Basement and garage. Sold by home centers and hardware stores. The wide blade is characteristic; sand shovels and grain shovels are so similar to snow shovels that they are interchangeable.

Primary
Uses:

Moving heavy snow off the sidewalk and driveway. Moving sand, wheat, and other granular materials.

Operating
Principle:

Stance is everything when moving materials with a shovel. Get it right and you can move tons with hardly any actual lifting—just push, pivot, and slide.

Variations:

Snow pushers are long-handled shovels with very wide blades for pushing snow into a heap that can be removed with the snow shovel.

Safety Note: Snow shoveling by unfit persons brings on more back injuries and heart attacks than any other activity. You can always phone somebody in the snow-plowing business. (Look up landscapers in the yellow pages— it's what they do in winter.)

How to Use: 1.   **Put on work boots and work gloves.**

2.   **Take a marching stance and hold the snow shovel with both hands, one hand on the D handle and the other on the shaft.**

3.   **Lean forward from the waist so the shovel's blade is parallel to the ground and thrust the blade under or into the pile of snow. Push it from the D handle. If the snow is crusty, rock the handle up and down to break it.**

4.   **With your lower hand as the fulcrum and the handle as the lever, lift the shovelful of snow until it just clears the snow pile. Do not tilt the shovel or the snow will slide off.**

5.   **Straighten your back, then pivot from the feet (not from the hips) toward the delivery zone to unload. One way to unload is to twist the handle so the snow falls off. Another way is to tilt the blade so the snow slides off.**

Tool-Kit
Minimum:

In snow-prone areas, one shovel is essential. Keep an additional snow shovel and a sack of coarse sand or dry cat litter in the car trunk.

51. **SNOW THROWER**

General
Description:

A gasoline engine on two fat, knee-high wheels with motorcycle-style handles sticking up from one side, a large opening near the ground on the side opposite the handles, and an adjustable chute poking into the air. The large opening, or mouth, contains a spiral reel of metal vanes that rotates when the engine is running. The upright discharge chute contains a small, rapidly spinning propeller. The engine housing also carries an electric starter, two filler caps (one for regular gas and the other for engine oil), an engine priming button, and a choke. The handle controls include a clutch and gearshift for the powered wheels, plus a speed control for the snow-eating reel.

Habitat:

Garage and garden shed. Sold by home centers and power equipment specialists. The large mouth, reel, and upright discharge chute distinguish it from lawn mowers and other yard machines.

Primary
Use:

Clearing snow off driveways, sidewalks, and paths.

Operating
Principle:

The auger. A rotating reel is, in effect, an auger or endless belt. Shoving it into a bed of snow pulls the snow into the machine's maw, and moving forward delivers more snow. A pair of adjustable skids control how close to the ground the thrower operates; rough surfaces such as gravel require a higher setting.

Variations:

Small, electrically powered snow throwers combine reel and impeller in one device. Low-priced gasoline-powered snow throwers do not have electric starters, which are essential in cold temperatures. Larger snow throwers have tank treads instead of wheels, while the largest are ride-on machines like yard tractors. Some yard tractors have snow-throwing attachments.

Safety Note:

It is never safe to reach inside the snow-thrower's mouth or discharge chute while the motor is running. If the chute clogs with icy snow, disengage the engine before you break up the clog by poking it with a stick or pry bar, never with your hand or foot.

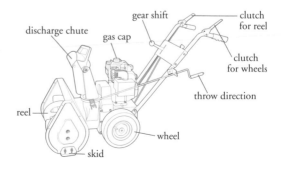

How to Use: 1. **Choose a snow thrower whose width and engine power match the area to clear. Put on your boots, gloves, winter hat, and hearing protectors. Top off the gas tank and check the oil.**

2. **Start the snow thrower's engine and drive it into the snow. Adjust the engine speed and forward speed to match the depth and weight of the snow: slower for deeper and heavier, faster for light and fluffy. Adjust the chute to throw the snow where you want.**

3. **To clear a sidewalk, start at one end and march to the other, throwing the snow to the downwind side.**

4. **To clear a driveway, make the first swath down the middle, throwing the snow to the downwind side. Then make repeat passes alongside the opening swath, always throwing the snow to the nearest side, until you reach the driveway's edges.**

5. **To clear a dense berm of ice left in your driveway by the town plow, nibble an opening across the berm, then enlarge it by making narrow, crosswise passes, switching the direction of the wheels from forward to reverse as needed. Direct the discharge chute to either side, not into the street.**

6. **At the end of the snow season, drain the gas tank or run it dry, which will make the engine more likely to**

start when you need it next. Hose it off to remove
road salt.

Tool-Kit
Minimum:
While you could clear any amount of snow with a
snow shovel, it is easier and faster with a snow thrower.

52. **SPADE**

General
Description:
*A long and sturdy wooden handle with a metal blade
socketed onto one end.* The head-sized blade is straight
across its top edge, with side edges that curve to a
broad point. The blade itself curves from side to side,
and it meets the handle at a small angle, not in-line.
With its blade pointed at the earth, the spade's handle
ends about chin high.

When used along with the pick, the spade is the
premier device for the strenuous labor of digging
holes. Observers who misconstrue the spade as a
device for propping up lazy laborers reveal their lack
of experience using one—it's hard and dirty work that
can't be done without resting.

Habitat:
Garden shed or garage. Sold by home and garden
centers. Distinguish the spade from the hoe by its
larger, slightly cranked blade.

Primary
Uses:
Turning the soil to prepare beds for planting. Digging
holes in the earth. Lifting loose material out of holes.

Operating Principle:	The design of the shovel harnesses the power of the back, hips, and legs to thrust downward. The blade's angled nose and thin cross-section allow it to cut the earth like a knife, versus the pick, which is a raw club.
Variations:	Gardeners may prefer a short, D-handled shovel with a square end, especially good for cutting turf and edging planting beds. Infantrymen and campers carry a short folding spade they call an "entrenching tool." The garden trowel is a small one-handed spade. A posthole digger is a pair of narrow spades facing one another, connected by a pivot.

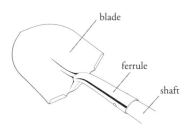

blade

ferrule

shaft

How to Use:

1. Put on work gloves and heavy boots.

2. Set the spade's point on the edge of the future hole.

3. Grasp the top of the spade's handle, then lift your dominant foot and plant it on the rolled metal at the top of the blade.

4. Rock your body forward and simultaneously thrust the spade downward with your foot. Use your body weight along with the muscles in your back and legs. The spade should cut into the earth, unless it hits a rock, in which case move and try again.

5. Lever the spade's handle down toward the ground so the blade lifts and breaks the soil.

6. When you're done for the day, clean the spade by shoving its blade into a bucket of sand, or rinse it off with water.

Note: To lift debris out of a deep hole, stand down in it. Hold the spade's handle by its end and center, then lean to shove its blade underneath the loose material. With your forward hand as a stationary fulcrum, push downward on the spade's handle to lift the blade-load of debris out of the hole, then twist the handle to dump the debris alongside the hole.

Tool-Kit Minimum: A spade is the only nonmechanized way to dig a serious hole in the ground.

53. 📷 **SPREADER**

General Description: *A knee-high metal hopper with two wheels and a handlebar.* A small gate in the bottom of the hopper may be opened and shut by working a lever on the handle-bar. Directly below the gate is a small propeller that goes around when you turn the wheels or push the contraption forward.

Habitat: Garden shed and garage. Sold by home and garden centers. The arrangement of hopper, adjustable gate, and propeller is enough for positive identification.

Primary Uses: Spreading grass seed and soil nutrients over a lawn. Distributing deicing agents on slippery walks and driveways.

Operating Principle: A small gear train transfers the motion of the wheels to the propeller, which bats into whatever granular material falls through the gate.

How to Use: 1. **Close the gate while you fill the hopper. The seed or fertilizer package might provide information about how densely it should be spread, which translates to how wide you open the gate.**

2. **Determine how far to either side the spreader throws its contents, and use that information to choose your starting point.**

3. **Push the spreader across the area until you have broadcast its contents everywhere.**

4. **Rinse the spreader before you store it away. This is critical if you have been spreading deicing materials, which otherwise would corrode the mechanism.**

Tool-Kit
Minimum:

Unnecessary until you seed a lawn. Once you have it, you'll wonder how you ever melted ice off the driveway without it.

---

54. 📷 **STRING TRIMMER**

General
Description:

A small gasoline or electric motor mounted on one end of a stiff, person-long wand with a rotating hub sprouting two short, nylon strings mounted on the other end. Close inspection reveals a throttle and carrying handle. A flat shield is located around the shaft, above the string hub, with a sharp metal blade on its rim.

Habitat:

Garden shed or garage. Sold by home centers and power equipment dealers. The engine and hub sprouting two nylon strings is positive identification.

Primary
Use:

Trimming grass and weeds. The string trimmer is the powered alternative to grass clippers.

Secondary
Uses:

Mowing rough and rocky fields. When equipped with a saw blade instead of a string head, cutting brush.

Variations:

Wheeled models operate like lawn mowers.

How to Use: 1. **Check the string trimmer's fuel level and top off if necessary. Put on hearing protectors and safety glasses.**

2. **Start the engine. Fit the strap over your shoulders and grip the wand and handle with both hands. Bump the hub on the ground to advance fresh string; the blade on the safety guard automatically cuts it.**

3. **Move the rotating string hub into the vegetation you want to cut. Long stems are liable to tangle the trimmer's mechanism, so tall grass and weeds are best felled by lowering the trimmer into them and chopping from the top down.**

Note: **Don't allow the trimmer to whip into tree trunks; it will damage the bark.**

Tool-Kit Minimum: Not as useful as hedge shears (page 82); best when you have a lot of edge to trim.

55a–b. **TROWEL**

General Description: *A hand-sized wooden or plastic handle mounted in line with a hand-sized blade that tapers to a point.* In both size and general purpose, the steel blade of the trowel stands in perfectly for your soft fingers when you want to make holes in the ground; if you had a steel hand you probably wouldn't need a trowel.

Habitat:	Garden shed and garage. Sold by home and garden centers. Distinguish the trowel from the spade by its very small size, otherwise they are similar.
Primary Use:	Digging and refilling holes to plant seeds and bulbs.
Secondary Uses:	Sculpting sand mermaids on the beach.
Variations:	Hand-sized forks, rakes, and cultivators are often packaged with trowels in matched sets. Mason's trowels have a flat, diamond-shaped blade.

How to Use:

1. **Hold the garden trowel in one hand as if it were a kitchen spatula.**

2. **Set the point of the trowel inside the future hole and push the trowel into the soil; scoop soil from the hole, and dump it to one side.**

3. **Put the trowel down while you plant the bulb or seed. Pick up the trowel to refill the hole by scraping up the soil you dumped in Step 2.**

4. **Rinse the trowel in water when you are done.**

Tool-Kit Minimum:	A trowel was probably your first gardening tool, for your first potted plant.

V. Electrical and Electronic

Modern homes are virtually draped in electrical cables, telephone wires, coaxial TV cable, speaker wire, and computer connections. All this wiring consists of metal conductors inside plastic insulating sleeves for carrying electrical impulses of various kinds. Choose the right kind of wire, run and install it from source to destination, then make the appropriate connections at either end to operate all your electronics.

56a–b.

ELECTRICAL PLIERS

General Description:

Steel tool with two colorful plastic handles, short jaws, and a tightly machined joint. Opening the handles opens the jaws, which are square and rough at the ends, with sharp cutting edges between the square ends and the joint. On the handle side of the joint, a little nib of metal sticks into a corresponding slot; some linesman's pliers have a second pair of roughened surfaces just above the handles.

Electrical pliers are for working with household electrical wire. The sharp portion of the jaws is a wire cutter. The little nib of metal is for crimping terminal lugs onto the ends of the wire. When you close the pliers, note that the sharp wire-cutting jaws meet together but there's always a little space between the square, rough-surfaced jaws. That's because you want the pliers to grip electrical wire, but not to crush it or flatten it.

Habitat: Toolbox of mechanic and electrician. Sold by hardware stores, home centers, and auto parts stores. The combination of tightly machined knuckle, toothy jaws, and built-in wire cutter with insulated handles is positive identification.

Primary Uses: Pulling, bending, twisting, and cutting household electrical wire.

Secondary Uses: Pulling, bending, twisting, and cutting any mechanical parts that will fit within the pliers' jaws.

Operating Principle: Long handles and short jaws give the pliers leverage. Electrical wire made of copper is softer than steel, so rough or toothy jaws can get a grip on it.

Variations: Needlenose electrical pliers have the same characteristics as linesman's pliers, except the jaws are long and thin for reaching deep into electrical boxes and making tight loops in the ends of the wire. Hobby pliers look like electrical pliers except they have smooth jaws for working with delicate materials such as floral wire.

How to Use: 1. **Hold the linesman's pliers in your dominant hand with one handle nestled in your palm near the base of** the thumb and the other against your first three fingers. Slip your pinky between the handles.

2. To cut electrical wire, bed it in the jaws as close to the pliers' knuckle as possible. Then squeeze the handles tight together.

3. To pull wire through studs or conduit, close the pliers on the end and twist them to make a bend, then pull against the bent portion.

4. To twist the ends of two pieces of wire together, hold them side by side and grasp them loosely in the jaws of the pliers. Then twist the pliers around the wires, allowing them to slip in the jaws. Continue until you achieve the desired result.

Tool-Kit Minimum: One pair of 9-inch (23 cm) electrical pliers will prove handy in many situations, not all of them electrical.

---

57. **OUTLET TESTER**

General Description: *A finger-sized piece of plastic sprouting short red and black wires, both ending in pointy metal probes.* A little window in the plastic part houses a tiny lightbulb.

Habitat: Electrician's toolbox. Sold by hardware stores and home centers. The minimal form—a tiny lightbulb in a finger of plastic, and red and black probes—is characteristic of an outlet tester.

Primary
Use:

Safely learning whether an electrical outlet has electricity in it. Contrary to popular practice, the index finger is not a suitable probe.

Secondary
Uses:

Electricians call them "continuity checkers" and use them to confirm the presence of electrical current at switches, light fixtures, and other devices in a circuit.

Operating
Principle:

An electrical current flowing through a loop of wire creates a visible glow in a little lightbulb when connected in-line with the electrical current. The connection is made when you plug the probes of the tester into an electrical outlet.

Variations:

Some outlet testers have a fat plastic body with three tiny lights and a three-prong plug that matches standard electrical outlets; these can't check loose wires, switches, or two-prong outlets. A printed key explains what each combination of lights indicates.

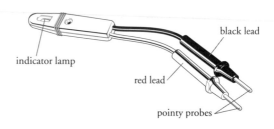

indicator lamp

black lead

red lead

pointy probes

How to Use: 1. **Select the outlet to check. When troubleshooting a household circuit, start closest to the main electrical panel.**

2. **If it's a two-prong outlet, insert one of the probes into one side of it, then poke the other probe into the other side. If it's a three-prong outlet, insert one of the probes into the centered round opening. Then poke the other into one of the straight openings.**

3. **Look at the lightbulb on the outlet tester. If it glows, the outlet is connected to electricity. If it doesn't glow, and the outlet is two-pronged, there's no electricity. If the outlet is three-pronged and the bulb doesn't glow, repeat the test using the other of the straight openings. If the outlet is working correctly, the tester will glow when connected one way but not when connected the other way. If you get a glow either way, or no glow either way, the outlet is not correctly connected.**

58. **SOLDERING GUN**

General Description: *A black plastic "pistol" with a red trigger, a fat barrel, and an electrical cord.* Two shiny electrodes extend from the barrel; they're connected by an H-shaped loop of copper wire called a "soldering tip." A close look reveals a splash of a silvery metal called "solder" coating the copper at the very end of the tip. If you plug in the device and pull the trigger, the device buzzes softly and the copper tip quickly becomes hot.

Habitat: Electrician's toolbox, workbench of electronic, audio, or video hobbyist. Sold by hardware stores and electronics specialty shops. The black plastic pistol with electrodes and a soldering tip is characteristic.

Primary
Uses: Making a strong, unambiguous electrical connection between two copper wires twisted together, or between a wire twisted onto the terminal of an electrical device. Repairing jewelry.

Operating
Principle: Electrical resistance in a wire manifests itself as heat. The connection is made when electricity heats the soldering tip, the tip heats the wires, the hot wires melt the solder, the molten solder flows into the spaces among the twists and solidifies.

Variations: Fancy soldering guns have little headlights to help you see small connections. The low-budget tool for soldering wires is called a "pencil iron"; it plugs in but takes a while to heat up and has no on/off trigger. Leaded-glass artists use a soldering iron with a substantial tip ideal for delivering heat to larger masses of metal.

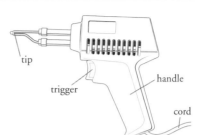

How to Use: 1. With a wire cutter, strip insulation off the ends of the wires to be joined.

2. Plug the soldering gun into an electrical outlet. Uncoil a short length of solder. Solder for electronics comes in spools; the solder forms a hollow tube surrounding a chemical called "flux" that helps the solder flow.

3. Grasp the handle of the soldering gun in one hand, the coil of solder in the other.

4. Touch the future connection with the soldering tip. Squeeze the trigger and hold it long enough to heat the wires.

5. Touch the hot wires with the free end of the solder. If the wire is hot enough, the solder will abruptly melt. It's very important to melt the solder by heating the wires. If you melt it directly with the soldering tip,

you're liable to create a "cold joint," which will be fragile and won't properly conduct electricity. Cold joints, which are extremely difficult to detect and repair, are a common cause of failure in electronic equipment.

6. Release the gun's trigger as you remove both the soldering tip and the coil of solder.

---

59. [icon] **TELEPHONE JACK TOOL**

General
Description: *Two plastic handles connected by a pivot at one end.*
Telephone jack tools feature a small, square opening in one handle. Almost nothing happens when you squeeze the handles together, but a close look shows that a small piece of metal pushes into the square opening. A second opening houses a sharp blade.

Habitat: Found among telephone wires and equipment. Sold by telephone dealers and electronics specialty shops.

Primary
Use: Connecting telephones and related equipment by attaching plastic four-wire RJ-11 jacks (also called "plugs") on the ends of flat telephone wires. Running telephone wires all over your house.

Variations: The telephone and electronics industries manufacture connecting tools for every kind of plug or jack.

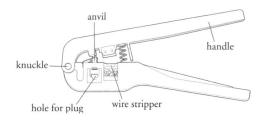

How to Use:

1. **Determine that you are dealing with standard, flat, four-wire telephone cable. If the wires are colored, the colors are black, red, yellow, and green. There may be a tiny spine or colored stripe on one flat side of the cable, which helps you orient the ends the same way.**

2. **Use wire cutters (page 128) to cut the cable straight across.**

3. **To strip the exactly right amount of insulation off the cable without damaging the wires inside, use the little blade in the telephone jack tool. Put the end of the cable into the opening that contains the blade, squeeze the handles together, and release. Turn the cable over, insert it, and squeeze again, but this time pull the wire out of the tool before you release the handles.**

4. **Insert a new, unused jack into the tool's socket.**

5. Insert the stripped wire into the flat hole in the end of the plug. If there's another plug on the other end of the cable, use the tiny orientation stripe to ensure both ends match. Push the cable into the plug as far as it will go.

6. Squeeze the handles together to make the connection. Release the handles, then press the toggle on the plug to release it from the tool.

Tool-Kit Minimum: When you're tired of long phone-cord tangles, you'll need a telephone jack tool.

60. **TV CABLE CRIMPER**

General Description: *A pliers-like tool with a hexagonal opening in its jaws.* The opening fits the end connectors on standard coaxial TV cable. Squeezing the handles crimps a connector onto the end of the cable. This is necessary whenever you want to add another television set or a high-speed Internet modem to the coaxial cable system in your house.

Habitat: Cable TV installer's tool belt, toolbox of electronic hobbyist. Sold by electronics specialty shops.

Primary Use: Capping the ends of TV cable so you can connect a TV set to an incoming cable jack or box.

Operating
Principle: TV cable, also called "coaxial cable," consists of a single small, stiff copper wire surrounded by white or clear plastic insulation that keeps it precisely centered in a flexible jacket braided from many fine wires.

Variations: Each size of coaxial TV cable requires its own connector, with its own crimping tool.

How to Use: 1.   **Verify that you are working with coaxial cable. Cut the end of the cable square across.**

2.   **Use pliers and a small knife to prepare the end of the cable by stripping a finger's width of black insulation.**

3.   **Fold the braided jacket back on itself, creating a collar around the protruding cylinder of insulation and the central copper wire.**

4.   **Fit the cable connector onto the end of the cable. Part of it will fit snugly around the braided collar. The copper wire should be visible in the connector.**

5.   **Fit the cable crimping tool onto the connector and squeeze its handles together.**

6.   **Release the crimping tool and test the cable by connecting an incoming TV signal to a television set. If it works, the connection is good. If not, cut the connector and try again.**

61. 📷 **WIRE CUTTER**

General
Description:

A pair of special pliers whose jaws come to a sharp edge and close in a tight V. The metal handles have colored plastic insulation and are also called "diagonal cutters."

Habitat:

Electrician's toolbox. Sold by hardware stores and home centers. The jaws butt together, and their sharp edges are in line with the handles, which offers positive identification (versus snips, whose sharp edges pass one another, and tile nippers, whose sharp edges run at right angles to their handles).

Primary
Use:

Cutting insulated and bare wire.

Operating
Principle:

To get more leverage on thick and tough wire, move the wire as deep as possible into the cutter jaws.

Variations:

Most of the pliers made for electrical work, as well as many general-purpose pliers, include a wire cutter. It's usually closest to the knuckle.

How to Use: 1.

Decide where you intend to cut the wire. Be conservative. It's easy to cut a longer length, but impossible to seamlessly attach a new piece.

2.

Open the jaws by opening the handles. Nestle the wire as deep as possible in the jaws.

3. **Close the cutters on the wire by squeezing the handles together.**

Tool-Kit
Minimum:

One pair of 8-inch (20 cm) wire cutters.

62a–d. ## WIRE STRIPPER

General
Description:

A pair of crossed metal handles connected by a pivot pin, with bypass jaws that have a sharpened notch where they meet. Close inspection reveals a spring for opening the jaws and a set screw in one handle for setting the precise size of the sharpened notch.

Habitat:

Electrical toolbox and workbench of computer, audio, or video hobbyist. Sold by hardware stores, home centers, and electronics specialty shops.

Primary
Use:

Removing a controlled length of insulation from the end of an electrical wire without nicking or damaging the copper conductors inside.

Variations:

Electronics technicians use a complex, double-action tool that simultaneously holds the wire and strips the insulation, with a row of notches for different-sized wires. Electricians use a small, sheet-metal tube with a sharp tab inside for slitting the outer insulation on large power cables.

How to Use: 1. Adjust the wire strippers so they'll cut through the insulation without nicking the copper wire inside.

2. Hold the wire strippers between the fingers and palm of one hand. Hold the wire to be stripped in the other.

3. Place the wire into the notch of the strippers. Squeeze the handles together.

4. Keeping the handles locked together, pull the wire out, leaving its insulation behind.

5. Examine the stripped wire to make sure it isn't nicked or scraped. If it is, adjust the strippers for a shallower bit and try again.

VI. Carpentry and Building

Building and carpentry are the arts of constructing shelters and making them fit for habitation. Site preparation (perhaps demolition), establishing a foundation, putting up walls and roofs, and making the whole thing weather-tight are just some of the issues a builder faces. Most amateur handypersons can easily perform general repairs to walls, floors, and roofs, plus install windows, doors, moldings, and appliances with a little experience.

63.   **AIR COMPRESSOR**

General Description:
An electrical motor mounted alongside a metal tank. A regulator apparatus with dials and knobs sprouts a single small nozzle. When you connect the electricity and switch the motor on, the air compressor runs for a while and then stops by itself. Squeezing the trigger on the nozzle uncorks a blast of air—and soon the motor starts up again. A coil of tight, hard, yet flexible air hose has end fittings that mate with the regulator and nozzle.

Habitat:
Builder's work sites, painter's truck, automotive repair shops, and well-equipped home workshops. The hollow metal tank with no apparent openings, along with the regulator gauges, confirms identification.

Primary Uses:	Spraying paint and lacquer. Energizing air-powered handheld tools such as drills, sanders, staplers, and nail guns, which are lighter and more efficient than electrical ones, but at the price of being tethered to the compressor by an air hose.
Secondary Uses:	Inflating automobile tires. Cleaning parts and dusty clothing by blasting them with compressed air.
Operating Principle:	An electrically driven piston can push a lot of air into a small tank. Releasing the air retrieves the energy that compressed it.
Variations:	Small units that intermittently drive nail guns may not be able to deliver the sustained pressure needed for spraying paint.

How to Use: 1. **Connect the hose from the regulator to the air hand tool and start the compressor.**

2. **Adjust the regulator to match air pressure to what the tool needs.**

3. **Squeeze the trigger to operate the tool.**

4. **Maintain the air compressor and clean its water filter on the schedule recommended by its owner's manual.**

64.   **AXE**

General
Description:

*A sharp, hand-sized wedge of iron attached to a stout
wooden handle.* The wedge tapers to a sharp, curved
edge. The handle has a graceful shape like the ankle
of a deer and plugs tightly in a socket, or eye, passing
through the iron wedge. The iron wedge is the head
or bit of the axe, the sharp part is its blade, and its
flat back is the poll.

The axe is the tool primeval—before it there were
only sticks and rocks, useful by themselves but nothing compared to the power and versatility unleashed
by joining them together. The axe has spawned a large
number of striking and cutting-by-striking tools,
among them the hammer, pick, hoe, and spade.

There's an old joke to the effect that an axe lasts
forever, you just replace the handle or the head,
whichever part breaks. But this ignores the subtle par-
ticularity of axes. You can replace the handle as often
as necessary, and it's still the same axe. This is not true
if something happens to the head. Sharpen it forever,
but if it breaks, you start over.

While you work the axe, it works you. With an
axe and not much else, a person can convert raw trees
into shelter and warmth and useful implements.
Meanwhile the axe hardens the skin of your hands,
strengthens your arms and back, roots your feet on
the earth, and shifts your point of view.

Habitat:	Garage or woodshed. Sold by hardware stores and home centers. The sharp, wedge-shaped bit, combined with the graceful shape of the handle, leads to positive identification.
Primary Use:	Felling trees by hand; splitting bolts of wood sawn from felled trees. Splitting kindling for the fireplace or barbecue. Hammering (with the poll) tent pegs.
Operating Principle:	The head of the axe is a heavy wedge, with its curved edge contributing a slicing action to the cut. The handle extends the length of the arm that swings it, multiplying the axe head's store of kinetic energy for instantaneous release when it slams into the target.
Variations:	Small axes are hatchets. Logger's axes have a double blade and straight handle. Mauls are thick and blunt.

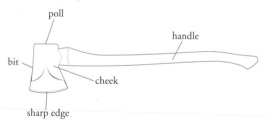

How to Use: **1. Choose an axe whose weight and length suit your own frame. Wear your steel-toed workboots and your safety glasses while you swing the axe to see how it feels, as well as when you work with it.**

2. To split a bolt (or block) of wood, stand it up on another, larger bolt (called the "chopping block"). Grasp the axe in two hands, take a marching stance, and swing overhead so the blade smashes straight down into the end of the target. If the wood splits, proceed to the next bolt. If not, wrench the axe loose and swing it again.

3. To sharpen an axe, file (page 283) the blade on both sides. Then use a sharpening stone (page 228) to remove the file marks.

65. **BELT SANDER**

General Description: *An electric motor atop a continuous, abrasive-coated belt driven by rollers fore and aft.* The sanding belt is as wide as your hand, and the complete contraption is as long as your forearm. A dust collection bag comes off one side of the belt sander; one of the two handles has an on/off trigger inside it. When you plug the sander in and pull the trigger, the machine makes a loud whirring noise, and the sanding belt speeds around the rollers. If you were to put the belt sander on the floor belt-side down, it would scoot forward under its own power like a crazed animatronic beast. Belt sander races across the subflooring are not unknown on building sites.

Habitat:	Builder's toolbox. Sold by home centers and tool specialists. The two wide rollers with two handles are definitive, whether or not there's an abrasive belt.
Primary Use:	Sanding floors, stairs, and trim to make the wood level and smooth before applying a finish.
Secondary Uses:	Leveling and cleaning up rough wood constructions. Grinding off square corners. Shaping wooden parts. Sanding old paint to prepare for repainting. Leveling welds and fiberglass patches for auto body repairs.
Operating Principle:	When hard and sharp grains of sand rub on a softer material such as wood, the soft material will weather into dust. Coarse abrasive sand (grits 36 through 80) cuts deeper and quicker than fine (grit 100 and up).
Variations:	Some metal-working sanders have a long, narrow abrasive belt. Some professional floor-sanding machinery has a very wide belt.
How to Use: 1.	**Choose a problem the belt sander can solve, bearing in mind that it is not a precision tool.**
2.	**Follow the sander's manual to install a belt whose fineness (grit) matches the task, with 36-grit or 40-grit for rough removal and 150-grit for final sanding before applying finish.**

3. Grasp the belt sander by both handles. Turn it on while holding it in the air, then gently lower it onto the workpiece.

4. Keep the sander moving under its own weight. Cover the entire surface evenly, paying particular attention to high or rough spots. Take care not to tip the sander up on edge, as that digs a deep gouge. If you dwell on any one spot, you'll sand it too low.

5. Progress through the available grits, from coarse to fine. Sand the entire surface before changing grits. Brush the dust off the surface as you work, and vacuum it up when you change grits.

6. Sanding old paint is likely to clog the belt. With the sander turned off, you can knock paint off the belt with a stiff wire brush.

---

66. **BIT BRACE**

General Description:

A cranked metal arm with what looks like a doorknob on one end and an intricate socket on the other. The handle spins freely, as does a second handle wrapped around the center of the crank. The socket part, or chuck, can be rotated, changing the opening size. A ratchet mechanism allows the brace to turn the chuck in one direction and not in the other.

The bit brace is a very old tool, now largely supplanted by the cordless electrical drill. The bit brace remains in use on job sites where there's no electricity for recharging batteries, in situations where the operator needs maximum control, and whenever one has an old-style auger bit of some particular size with no corresponding bit for power drills.

Habitat: Deep inside the builder's toolbox and woodworker's shop. Sold by hardware stores and home centers. Abundant at flea markets.

Primary Uses: Drilling holes in wood by muscle power. Driving screws into wood. Winding coils of wire.

Operating Principle: The lever—that is, the crank in the handle—allows the operator to apply a lot of force to the bit with each turn of the brace.

Variations: Angle braces can drill into inaccessible spots.

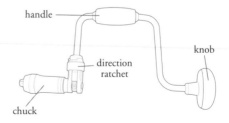

handle

knob

direction ratchet

chuck

How to Use: 1. Choose an auger bit or drill bit that matches the size of the future hole.

2. Open the chuck so it admits the tang of the bit, then tighten the chuck on it.

3. Clamp the workpiece to something solid, locate the center of the future hole, and make a dimple there (see awl, page 186).

4. Set the point of the bit on the dimple and position the brace so it is square to the surface. Put one hand on the doorknob handle and the other on the crank handle.

5. Press down on the doorknob while turning the crank. One direction advances the bit into the wood, the other retracts it.

6. If anything impedes making a complete turn (or sweep) of the crank, use the ratchet mechanism to advance the bit with partial sweeps.

7. Most bits lift their own waste, but sometimes you have to back out, clear chips, and resume.

Note: The bit makes a ragged exit hole. To avoid this, notice when the point first breaks through and retract the bit, then resume drilling from the back.

Tool-Kit
Minimum:

When the flea market presents a brace that feels good in your hand, give it a new home.

67a–b.

CAULK GUN

General
Description:

A sheet-metal half cylinder about the diameter of your wrist and the length of your forearm with a rod emerging from the end. The caulk gun features a spring and a metal bar wrapped around the rod, which is about as fat as a pencil and has a bend near the end. Squeezing the handle advances the rod and makes a clicking sound. There's a U-shaped cutout in the far end of the half cylinder.

Habitat:

Toolbox of carpenter, mason, or painter. Sold by home centers and hardware stores. Usually found with cardboard or plastic cartridges of caulk or adhesive.

Primary
Uses:

Applying beads of caulk along seams and cracks to waterproof and keep weather out or to prepare for painting. Applying beads of construction adhesive to boards and panels.

Variations:

Some caulk guns have notches all along the rod, another way of making the mechanism advance.

How to Use: 1.

Choose an empty caulking gun whose size matches your cartridge.

2. Cut the end of the cartridge's nozzle at an angle. Poke a long nail or a skewer into the nozzle to break its seal.

3. Fully retract the rod of the caulking gun and drop the cartridge into the gun's half cylinder. The nozzle drops into the U-shaped cutout.

4. Squeeze the handle to advance the rod until a blob of caulk oozes through the nozzle.

5. Position the blob at one end of the crack. Squeeze the handle as you smoothly move the nozzle along the crack.

6. Sometimes it works better to pull the bead, other times to push it ahead.

Tool-Kit Minimum: Drafty around that window? Caulk it tight.

---

68. **CHALK REEL**

General Description: *A lozenge of aluminum, hollow like a can and about hand sized, with a crank on one flat side and a little metal hook coming out of one end.* The hook has an eye tied to a piece of string that disappears into the can. Also known as a chalk reel, chalk box, or chalk line, this tool has a plastic window but colored dust blocks the view.

Dusty chalk is packed around a reel wound full of string. Along with the level and the plumb bob, the reel of string is one of those exquisitely elegant tools that's been with us since the beginning of civilization. It enables the creation of square corners and long, straight lines.

A string under tension describes a straight line. But a relaxed string is flexible—you can fold it and tie knots in it. So tie knots one-for-one to record a count, or tie them carefully spaced to record lengths. Thus the humble piece of string lies at the root of counting, measuring, and layout.

Habitat: Carpenter's toolbox and mason's truck. Sold by hardware stores and home centers. Usually there's a plastic bottle of colored chalk powder nearby.

Primary
Uses: Marking long, straight lines that can also, if you choose, be level. Builders do this first to create straight walls, then to establish level lines on them for installing pipes, paneling, doors and windows, tile, counters, siding, shingles, and trim.

Secondary
Uses: Drawing perfect hopscotch layouts on the sidewalk. To record a length, tie a pair of knots in the string. To find square, follow the lead of Pythagoras and mark out a 3-4-5 triangle using a knotted string and sticks.

Variations: Old-timers prefer to drag loose string across a lump of soft chalk. Japanese carpenters drag string from a reel through an inky wad in a carved wooden bowl called a *sumitsubo*—it snaps a crisp, black, and permanent line. Instead of a hook, the line ends with a sharp little awl that can be anchored anywhere.

How to Use: 1. **Locate one end of the future straight line.**

2. **Snag the hook on a point if one exists, or set an awl and catch the hook on that.**

3. **Pull the chalk reel to the other end of the future line, unrolling the string.**

4. **Hold the string taut with one hand and with two fingers of the other lift it off the surface. Let it go with a single quick pluck.**

5. **Unhook the chalk line and wind it up.**

Tool-Kit Minimum: You can mark a straight line on almost anything, including still water, with a chalk reel.

---

69. **DRILL, CORDLESS**

General Description: *A fat pistol made of colored plastic with a stubby barrel and an awkward, ungainly handle.* Cordless drills make for easy drilling without tangled cords. Without the connection to the wall, these tools resemble guns even more than their corded counterparts. If you squeeze the trigger, the device makes noise and the chuck at the end rotates.

Turning the collar shrinks and enlarges the opening of the chuck, and if you stick something in there, you can tighten the chuck around it. When you squeeze the trigger again, the inserted object rotates along with the chuck. The ungainly handle contains a removable object—the rechargeable battery. Once it has been removed, the drill no longer works.

Most cordless rechargeable drills have a switch for reversing the direction of rotation, with a speed control built into the trigger (squeeze more for faster, less for slower). Many also have a collar for adjusting the torque, or turning force.

Habitat: Toolbox of carpenter, builder, woodworker, or handyperson. Sold by hardware stores and home centers. Usually found along with drill bits and a battery charger. The pistol form with chuck is characteristic of drills, but positive identification is made difficult by the large variety of similar battery-operated portable tools available today.

Primary   Spinning drill bits in order to create a hole in wood,
Uses: metal, masonry, or plastic. Driving screws into wood, masonry, and metal.

Operating Principle: High-power rechargeable batteries liberated the electric drill from its power cord, no doubt contributing to the recent vast increase of holes drilled in awkward locations.

Variations: The bit brace (page 137) is the pre-electrical form. Small cordless drills may be configured in-line like screwdrivers, rather than like a pistol. Corded varieties are still common.

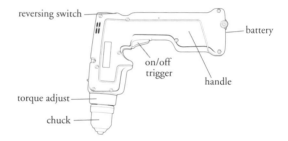

reversing switch

battery

on/off trigger

handle

torque adjust

chuck

How to Use:

1. **Choose a drill bit whose diameter matches the desired size of the future hole.**

2. **Locate and mark the center of the future hole.**

3. **Spin the collar to open the drill chuck and insert the drill bit. Spin the collar the other way to tighten the chuck on the shank of the bit. Squeeze the drill's trigger and observe the direction that the bit rotates.**

4. Wrap your hand around the grip. Set the point of the
    bit on the mark. Hold the apparatus upright so the
    drill bit makes a right angle with the surface sur-
    rounding the future hole. Wrap your other hand
    around the body of the drill to steady it and keep it
    lined up.

5. Squeeze the trigger to rotate the drill bit. Push the
    drill forward as it gnaws.

Note: If the bit spins without advancing into the hole or
        slows down and declines to spin, stop drilling and see
        if the bit is clogged with debris. If so, remove it
        before you resume drilling. If not, replace the battery.

Tool-Kit   Find a cordless drill whose heft and balance suits your
Minimum: hand and arm, and get a second battery to go with it.

70a–e.   **DRILL BITS**

General   *Intricately shaped steel cylinders ranging from finger*
Description: *length up to a full hand span, which, when rapidly*
                rotated, make holes in wood, metal, and plastic. Each
                drill bit makes one diameter of hole only, though the
                hole may vary in depth right up until it passes com-
                pletely through the workpiece (called a "through
                hole").

                Drill bits come in many varieties depending on

the size of the hole, the type of drilling equipment, and the material being drilled (wood, metal, plastic). All drill bits have common elements (tang, shank, sharp cutting lips), and while many of them twist, not all do. Begin by differentiating from router bits, which are short, thick, and do not have a center point. Next, determine which end of the bit does the cutting (it has sharp lips and a center point) and which end chucks into the drill, called the "tang." The shank is the smooth metal shaft in between. A square-tapered tang, like a tall pyramid, fits the chuck of a muscle-powered bit brace. Round and hexagonal shanks are meant for power drills, though they can be used in muscle-powered drills as well. The point at the other end, which may be threaded like a screw, is the bit's center, and it locates the center of the future hole. There are two different kinds of sharp edge. One type, called "spurs," cuts the perimeter of the future hole. The other type, called "lips," radiates from the bit's center point and sweeps out the area of the hole. The twisted part of the bit, called the "auger," lifts and ejects the chips severed by the spurs and peeled up by the lips.

It's dangerous to use a bit with a square tang and a threaded point in any machine-powered drill. Also, while not dangerous, it is ineffective to crank a flat spade bit in a muscle-powered drill. Small twist drills, whose lips slope to a shallow point, can be used in any drill and on almost any material.

Habitat: Builder's toolbox, woodworker's shop, and in large numbers and variety near drilling equipment. Sold by home centers and hardware stores. For guaranteed identification, find the tang, the shank, the spurs, the lips, and the center point. Small steel tools that don't have all of these parts probably are not drill bits.

Primary Use: Making holes in hard materials.

Variations: Adjustable bits for wood can be set to make holes of different sizes. Step drills for sheet metal drill increasingly large holes as they progress through the material. Tapered drills make holes that fit wood screws.

How to Use: 1. **Choose a bit whose diameter matches the desired size of the future hole, and whose shank matches your drilling equipment. Some bits have their size marked on the shank or tang and some don't; you can measure the bit with a caliper (page 190).**

2. **Clamp the bit in the drill chuck.**

3. **Locate and mark the center of the hole by punching or dimpling the workpiece. Clamp the workpiece to something solid.**

4. **Wear eye protection whenever you operate drilling equipment. Turn the drill on, align to the mark, then**

make contact. Use slow speeds for big holes, fast
speeds for small holes.

5. Observe the drill bit to make sure it is lifting the
   chips out of the hole. If not, pause and retract the bit
   to clear the chips.

6. Check the depth of the hole as you drill and stop
   before it's too deep.

Tool-Kit
Minimum: A set of twist drills for small holes, plus a larger set,
            that matches your drilling equipment.

71a–c. 📷   **HAMMER**

General   *A heavy lump of metal with one cylindrical end and the*
Description: *other divided into a claw that resembles two curving fin-*
              gers firmly attached to a stout, forearm-length handle. A
              hammer's metal head features a hole, or eye, into
              which the handle fits; the cylindrical end has a
              smooth, round face. The protruding handle comfort-
              ably fits in your hand, so wrap your fist around it.
              Feel the heft and see how it balances when you shift
              your grip along the handle. Turn it so the claw is on
              top. Find a block of wood and tap down on it with
              the face of the hammer. See how you can control the
              force of the blow. Now keep a firm grip on the handle
              and swing so the hammer's face hits the block of

wood. Note how it makes a dent, called a "hammer-track" or an "elephant-print." Hammer some more and feel the tension drain out of your body.

Habitat:	Builder's toolbox, kitchen tool drawer, and basement workbench. Sold by hardware stores and home centers. There are many kinds of hammers, but the flat face with two curved prongs on the back define the general-purpose claw hammer.
Primary Use:	Driving nails through one piece of wood and into a second piece to fasten them together. It takes at least three nails to make a firm connection, but too many is no better than too few.
Secondary Uses:	Driving wooden parts closer together or farther apart. Advancing such tools as chisels, pry bars, and center punches. Pulling nails (using the claw) from wood. Tapping walls to learn if they are hollow. Cracking nuts.
Operating Principle:	The metal head is like a heavy, armored fist and the handle increases leverage by making your arm longer.
Variations:	Claw hammers come in many sizes and weights. Framing hammers have a straight claw that carpenters use to help lift and move heavy planks. Mechanics and machinists prefer a ball in place of the claw. Upholsterer's hammers are small and light, with a nar-

row, straight claw that's magnetized for picking up
and starting tacks.

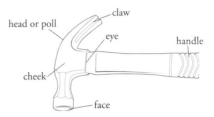

How to Use: 1. **Choose a hammer that feels right to you. Put on your safety glasses.**

2. **Locate and mark where the nail is to go.**

3. **Grip the hammer in your dominant hand.**

4. **Hold the nail upright on the marked spot, its point touching the wood. Hold it between thumb and fore-finger.**

5. **Use the face of the hammer to gently tap the nail enough so it stands up and you can get your fingers out of the way.**

6. **Shift your grip away from the hammer head, raise the hammer a little higher, and bring it down on the head of the nail. Observe the nail progressing into the wood.**

7.   **Repeat until the head of the nail is flush with the surface of the wood.**

Note: **Failing to remove your fingers from the vicinity of the nail ensures that you will hit them.**

Tool-Kit Minimum: Every household needs its own hammer.

72.   **HOLE SAW**

General Description: *A short, straight-sided cup of metal no bigger than your fist with sharp saw teeth all around its rim.* A drill bit sticks through the middle of the cup, which also has a hexagonal shaft on its back side.

Habitat: Carpenter's, plumber's, or electrician's toolbox, commonly in the company of an electric drill. Sold by hardware stores and home centers. The sawtooth cup and large size distinguishes it from drill bits; the cylindrical shape distinguishes it from other sawing tools.

Primary Use: Sawing holes in rough walls and floors so plumbing pipes and electrical wires can pass through. Installing knobs and locks in wooden doors.

Operating Principle: A piece of wood with a hole in it retains most of its strength, whereas one with a notch in the edge will be

Color Plates

1. **clamp**

2. **dust mask**

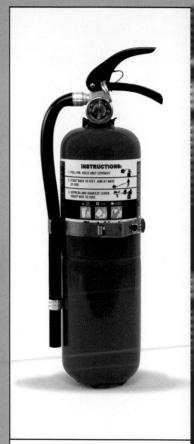

3. **fire extinguisher**

4. **gasoline can**

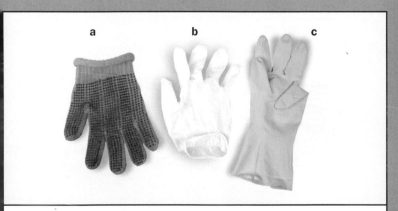

5. **gloves:** a) gardening; b) vinyl; c) rubber

6. **hearing protectors**

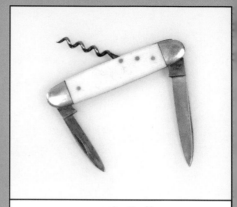

7. **pocketknife**

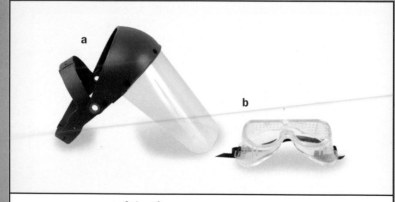

8. **safety glasses:** a) face shield; b) goggles

9. **work boot**

10. **bench brush**

11. **bucket**

12. **funnel**

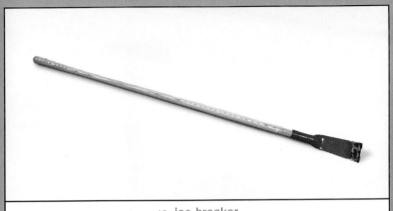

13. **ice breaker**

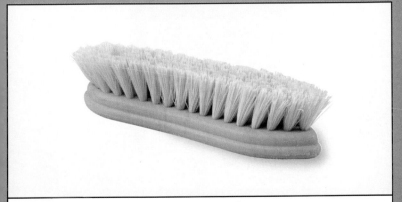

14. **scrub brush**

15. **shop vacuum**

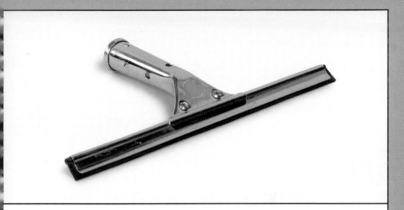

16. **squeegee**

17. **drywall knives:** a) new; b) vintage

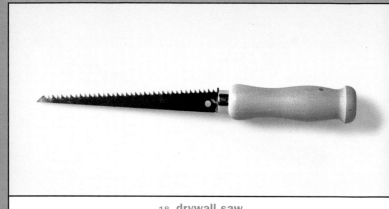

18. **drywall saw**

19. **glass cutter**

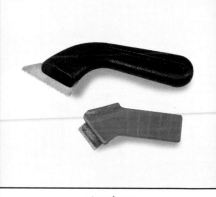

20. **grout saws**

21. hole punch

22. mastic trowel

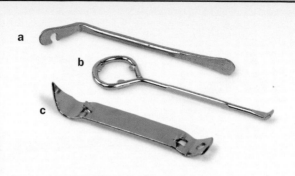

23. **paint can openers:**
a) opener and lifter; b) bottle and can opener; c) hook opener

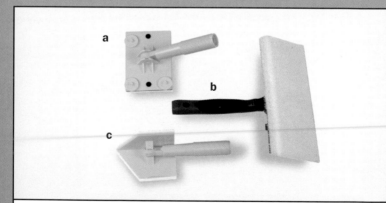

24. **paint pads:** a) trim; b) wall; c) corner

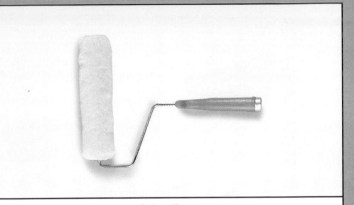

25. **paint roller**

26. **paintbrushes:** a) wall and siding; b) trim; c) chisel trim

27. putty knife

28. random orbit sander

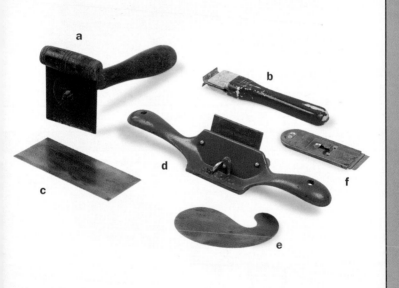

29. scrapers: a) floor scraper; b) paint scraper;
c) cabinet scraper; d) scraper plane; e) molding scraper; f) razor scraper

30. seam roller

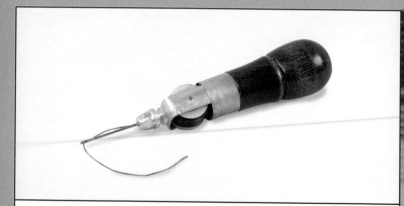

31. sewing awl

32. **stepladder**

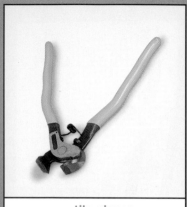

33. tile nipper

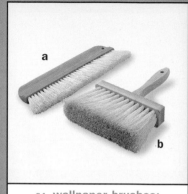

34. wallpaper brushes:
a) smoothing brush; b) paste brush

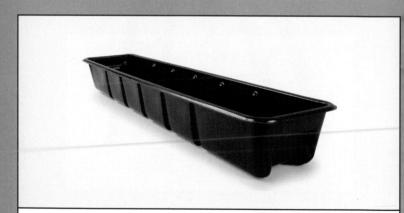

35. wallpaper trough

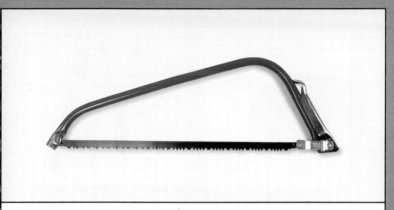

36. **bow saw**

37. **fork**

38. garden cart

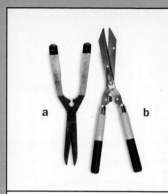

39. hedge shears:
a) vintage; b) new

40. hoe

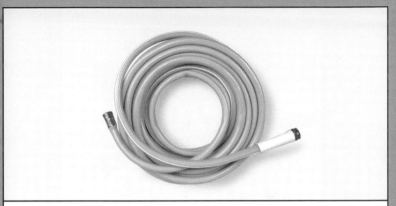

41. **hose**

42. **lawn mower**

43. leaf blower

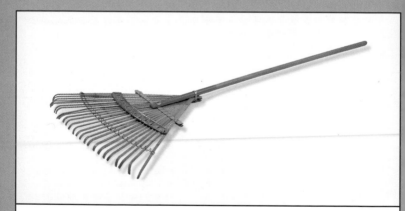

44. leaf rake

45. loppers

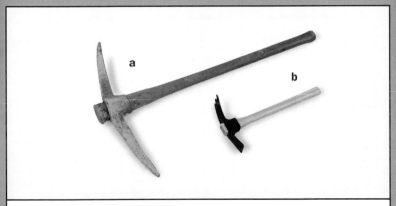

46. picks: a) standard pick; b) hand mattock

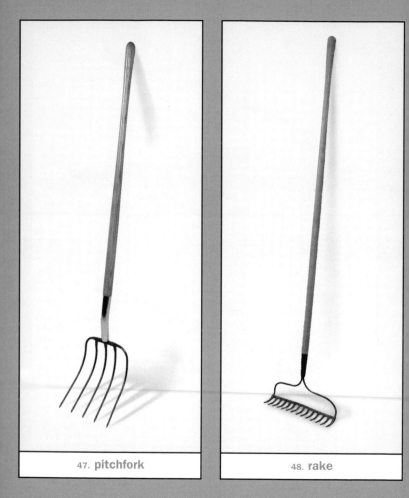

47. **pitchfork**

48. **rake**

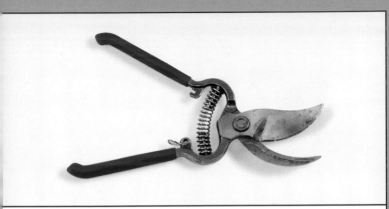

49. **secateurs**

50. **snow shovel**

51. snow thrower

53. spreader

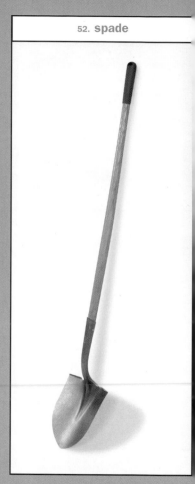

52. spade

54. **string trimmer**

55. **trowels:** a) garden trowel; b) mason's trowel

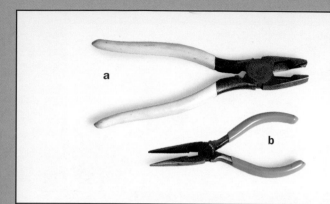

56. electrical pliers: a) linesman's pliers; b) needlenose pliers

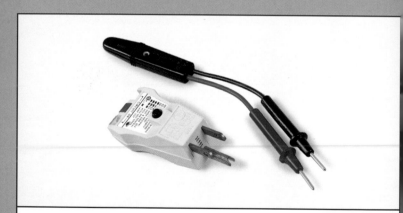

57. outlet testers

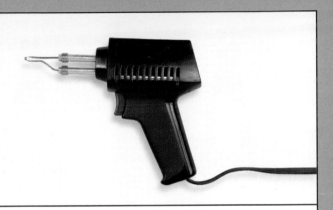

58. **soldering gun**

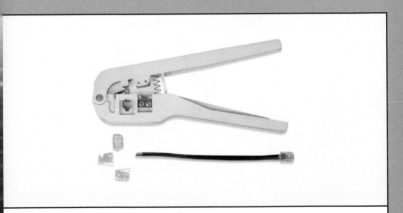

59. **telephone jack tool**

60. TV cable crimper

61. wire cutter

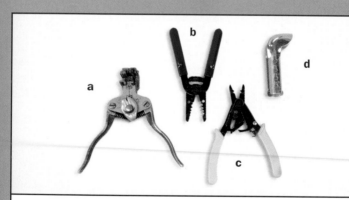

62. wire strippers: a) production wire stripper;
b) 4-size wire stripper; c) adjustable wire stripper; d) cable stripper

63. **air compressor**

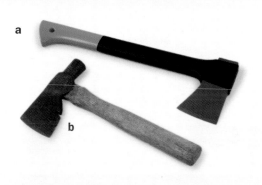

64. **axes:** a) firewood hatchet; b) roofer's axe

65. **belt sander**

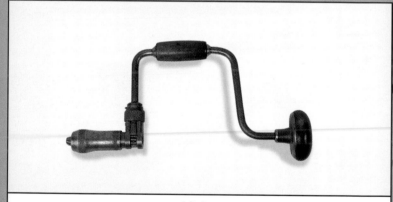

66. **bit brace**

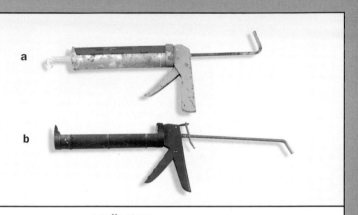

67. **caulk gun:** a) loaded; b) empty

68. **chalk reel**

69. **drill, cordless**

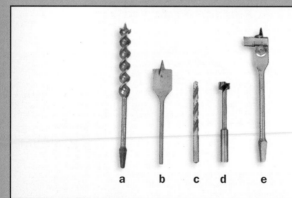

70. **drill bits:** a) auger; b) spade; c) twist; d) forstner; e) adjustable

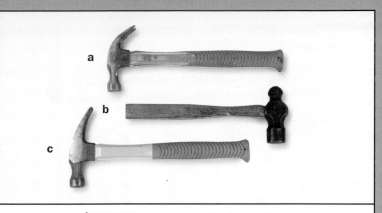

71. **hammers:** a) carpenter's; b) ball-peen; c) framing

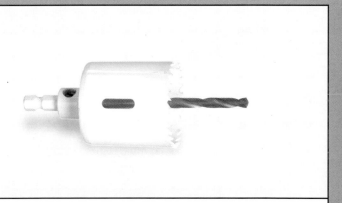

72. **hole saw**

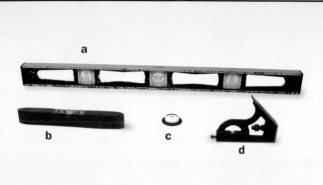

73. **levels:** a) beam; b) torpedo; c) bull's eye; d) combination square with level

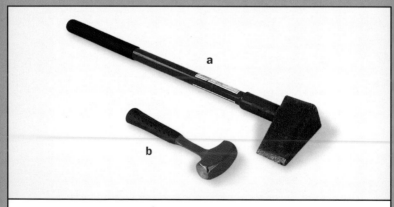

74. **mauls:** a) firewood; b) sledgehammer

75. plumb bob

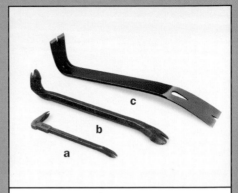

76. pry bars: a) nail puller;
b) cat's paw; c) flat bar

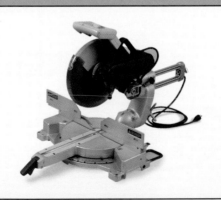

77. saw, chop

78. **saw, portable circular**

79. **saw, portable reciprocating**

80. **sawhorse**

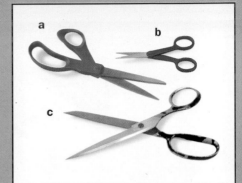

81. **scissors:**
a) paper; b) embroidery; c) dressmaker's

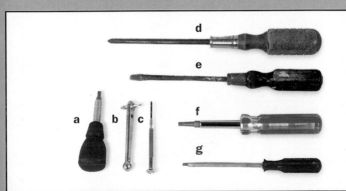

82. **screwdrivers:** a) stubby; b) right-angle;
c) camera/electronic; d) phillips; e) flat; f) torx; g) robertson

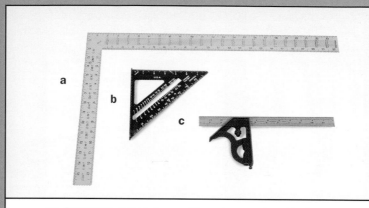

83. **squares:** a) framing square; b) speed square; c) combination square

84. **stud finder**

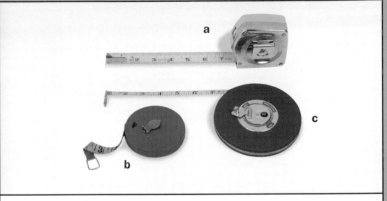

85. **tape measures:** a) builder's; b) cloth; c) site layout

86. **tie-down straps**

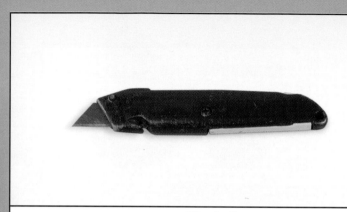

87. **utility knife**

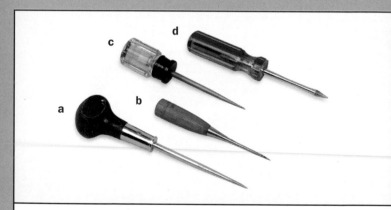

88. **awls:** a) scratch; b) japanese; c) stubby; d) gimlet

89. bevel gauge

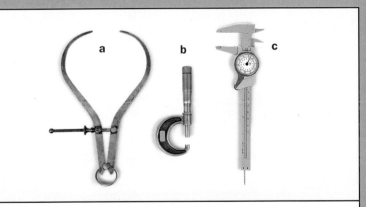

90. calipers: a) outside; b) micrometer; c) dial

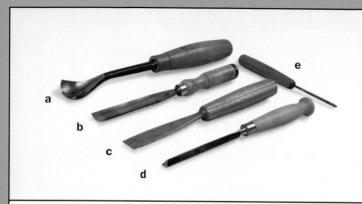

91. **carving tools:** a) spoon; b) sweep; c) skew; d) v; e) fluter

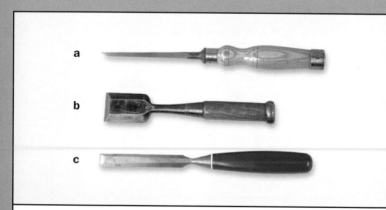

92. **chisels:** a) mortise; b) japanese; c) firmer

94. coping saw

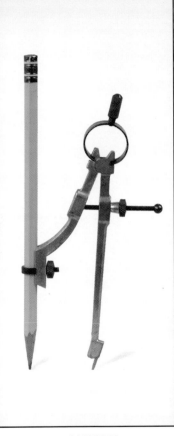

93. compass

95. hand drill

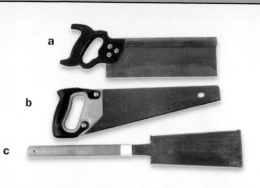

96. **handsaws:** a) backsaw; b) toolbox saw; c) ryoba (2-edge) saw

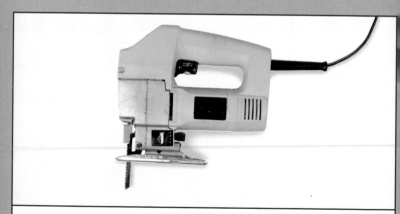

97. **jigsaw**

98. **magnifying glass**

99. **mallets:**
a) carver's; b) carpenter's

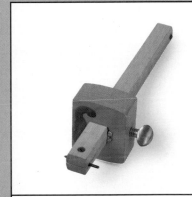

100. **marking gauge**

101. **plane**

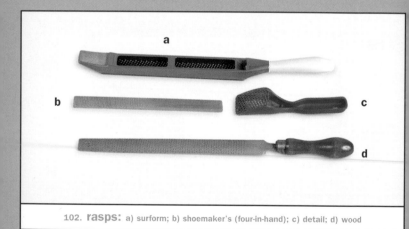

102. **rasps:** a) surform; b) shoemaker's (four-in-hand); c) detail; d) wood

103. router

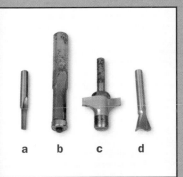

104. router bits:
a) straight; b) pilot bearing;
c) roundover; d) dovetail

105. sanding block

106. sharpening stones:
a) grinding wheel; b) slip; c) bench stone; d) diamond stone

107. table saw

108. **vise**

109. **workbench**

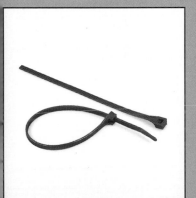

110. **cable ties**

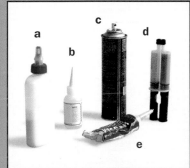

111. **glue:** a) yellow wood glue;
b) superglue; c) spray contact cement;
d) 2-part epoxy; e) silicone glue

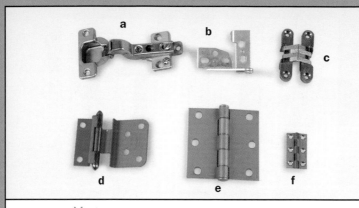

112. hinges: a) cup; b) knife; c) concealed; d) cabinet; e) butt; f) box

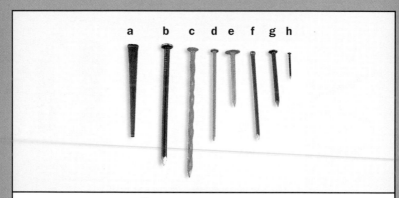

113. nails: a) cut; b) carpentry; c) screw floor;
d) box; e) roofing; f) finishing; g) marine; h) brad

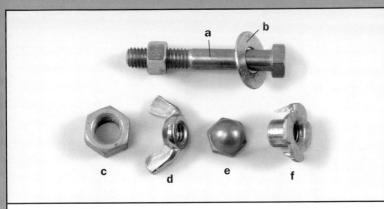

114. **nuts and bolts:** a) bolt; b) washer; c) hex nut; d) wing nut; e) cap nut; f) tee nut

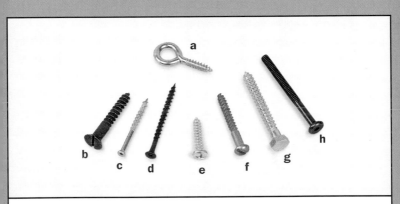

115. **screws:** a) eye; b) flathead; c) trim;
d) construction; e) sheet metal; f) round-head; g) lag; h) socket-head

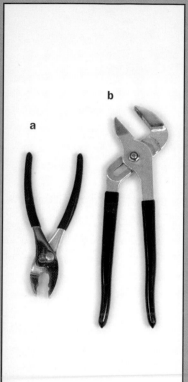

116. adjustable pliers:
a) slip joint; b) groove-joint

117. faucet puller

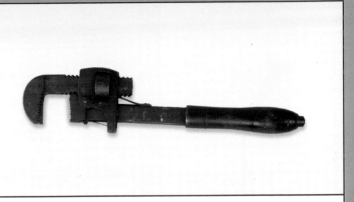

118. pipe wrench

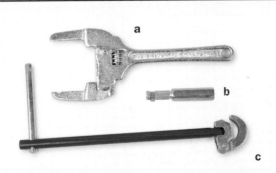

119. plumbing wrenches: a) flange wrench;
b) nipple wrench; c) crow's foot basin wrench

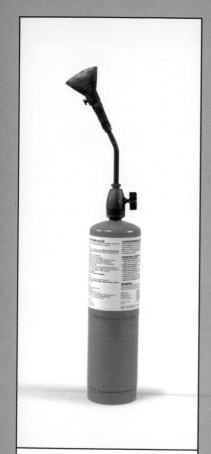

120. **propane torch**

121. **tubing cutter**

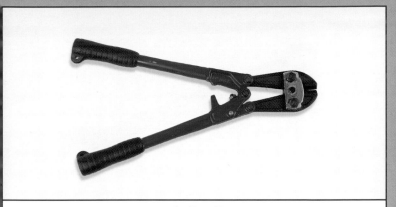

122. **bolt cutter**

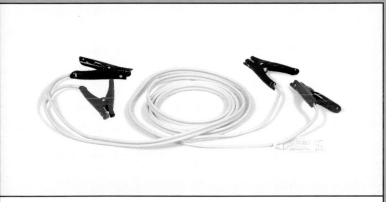

123. **booster cable**

124. **box wrench**

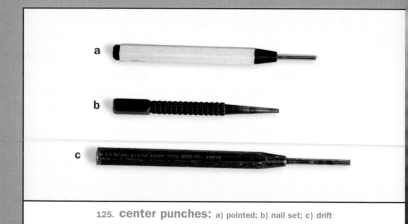

125. **center punches:** a) pointed; b) nail set; c) drift

126. **cold chisel**

127. **creeper**

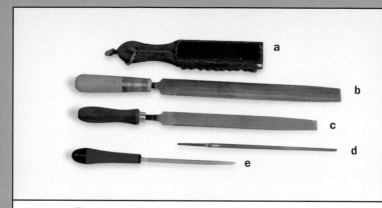

128. files: a) file card; b) half-round bastard; c) mill; d) round; e) triangular

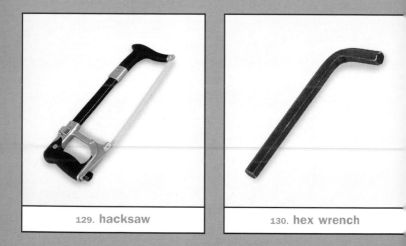

129. hacksaw

130. hex wrench

131. jack stand

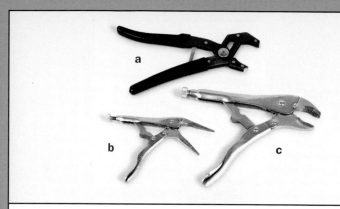

132. locking pliers: a) automatic; b) needlenose; c) standard

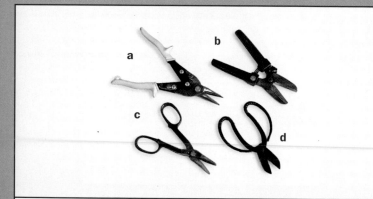

133. snips: a) aircraft; b) utility; c) tin; d) floral

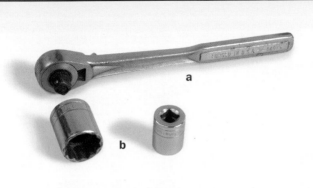

134. **socket wrench:** a) handle; b) socket

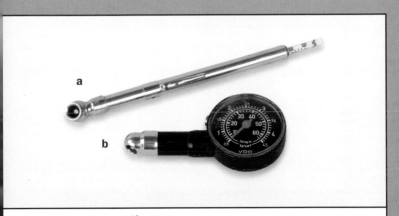

135. **tire gauges:** a) standard; b) dial

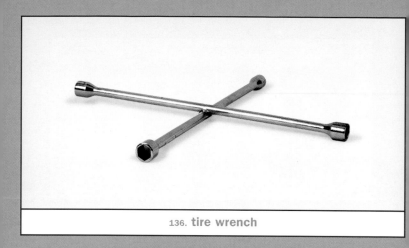

136. **tire wrench**

seriously weakened. This is why plumbers and electricians saw holes for pipes and wires through the middle of studs and joists even though it would be easier to saw notches.

Variations: Hole saws come in many sizes, from the diameter of your thumb up to the size of your closed fist; they're all long enough to saw through standard 2x lumber.

How to Use: 1. **Choose a hole saw whose diameter matches the desired size of the future hole.**

2. **Locate and mark the center of the hole.**

3. **Install the shank of the hole saw in the chuck of an electric drill. Pull the trigger to be sure it's plugged in or has a charged battery.**

4. **Set the point of the drill bit on the center of the future hole. Pull the trigger on the drill. Push the drill bit into the wood.**

5. **When the blade begins to cut, it will become difficult to advance. Retract the drill to clear the dust (swarf). Advance the saw by rocking the drill as you lean on it.**

6. **For a neat hole, stop when the drill bit begins to come through, remove the saw from the wood, and complete the drilling from the other side.**

7.   **When the saw breaks through, the disk of waste wood will begin to spin with it. Remove the saw and the waste wood from the hole.**

Note: **Most hole saws have slots into which you can insert a flat screwdriver for levering the waste out of the cup.**

Tool-Kit
Minimum: Acquire different-sized hole saws whenever you have different-sized holes to make.

73a–d. 📷   **LEVEL**

General
Description: *An aluminum bar about as long as your arm, with several small, clear windows set in it.* Each window of a level looks on a small, slightly curved vial of colored liquid with a single pea-sized bubble in it. Observe the bubble move as you move the body of the level.

People prefer flat and level floors not only because of their inner sense of balance, but also because stuff rocks around on lumpy surfaces and rolls downhill on slopes. Likewise doors, windows, furniture, and pictures: People are uncomfortable when their environment tilts.

Habitat: Toolbox of builder, carpenter, or mason. Sold by hardware stores and home centers. Often found with the chalk line and the plumb bob, the ancient trinity of layout tools.

Primary Use:	Learning whether a surface or an edge is level—that is, horizontal. Modern levels have two sets of vials at right angles to one another, so they may be used to test whether a surface is plumb, or vertical, as well.
Operating Principle:	Strictly speaking, "level" means tangential to the spherical surface of the earth, which is the same as intersecting squarely with a line drawn to the center of the earth.
Variations:	Levels come in a wide range of sizes, with 24 inches (60 cm) portable and common. Carpenters use a 4-foot (1.2 m) or 6-foot (1.8 m) level for door and window openings. A small bull's-eye level shows the direction of tilt. Many measuring devices incorporate a level, notably the surveyor's transit and the combination square. Many levels have built-in laser pointers that shine a bright and level line along the wall—in effect, they combine the level with the chalk line.
How to Use:	1. **Examine the level to determine which vial(s) indicate horizontal and which test for vertical.**
	2. **Place the level on the surface in question. Observe the appropriate bubble.**
	3. **If the bubble rises to the top center of the vial, the surface is horizontal in the direction of the level; skip to Step 5.**

4. **If the bubble remains off center, the surface slopes one way or the other. To determine which way it slopes and by how much, lift one end of the level and observe the bubble. When the bubble centers, you'll see by the space under the level which side of the surface to block up and by how much.**

5. **Turn the level 90 degrees on the surface in question and check again. It might be level one way but sloping in another. When the surface is truly horizontal, the bubble remains at top center no matter which way you turn it.**

Tool-Kit Minimum: A level settles all arguments about which is off-kilter, the picture or the critic.

74a–b. **MAUL**

General Description: *A large iron lump with a flat face at each end, attached to a stout wooden handle that's almost as long as your leg.* When you heft the maul you may be surprised by the weight of its iron head. If you attempt to wiggle the head on its handle, you'll find the attachment extremely secure—if not, the maul is defective and must not be used.

Habitat: Garage and builder's truck. Sold by hardware stores and home centers.

Primary Uses:	Demolishing buildings and breaking masonry. Driving stakes into the ground. Nudging heavy masses one way or the other. Splitting firewood. Breaking large rocks into smaller ones.

Operating Principle:	The momentum of, and kinetic energy transmitted by, a swinging hammer increases with the length of the handle, the weight of the head, and the velocity of the swing.

Variations:	The sledgehammer is a short-handled maul. Firewood mauls usually have a wedge on one end of the head, with a flat face on the other. Traditional timber carpenters shift posts and beams into place using large wooden mallets with iron-bound heads called "persuaders" or "commanders." Sometimes they persuade by swinging gently, like a croquet mallet, but when necessary a full overhand swing ultimately will prevail.

How to Use: 1. **Wear your work boots and heavy work gloves. Take a stable stance at a right angle to the workpiece, one foot planted in front of the other.**

2. **Stand the maul upright, head on the ground, and grasp its handle near the end.**

3. **Decide whether to take an overhand or underhand swing.**

4. **To gather momentum, use the full length of the handle but allow the weight of the maul to do much of the work—just accelerate it along its natural path until it strikes the target.**

---

75. **PLUMB BOB**

General
Description:

A heavy, finely made sharp-pointed metal teardrop with a string emerging from the center of the nonpointed end. Along with the chalk reel and the level, the plumb bob is ancient and elegant in its logical simplicity: The hanging weight pulls the string into alignment with gravity. It's used to test for vertical, but what it actually does is point directly toward the center of the earth. Builders regard verticality as essential when building upward, because things fall down when this relationship is ignored.

To find vertical, wait for the plumb bob to stop swinging. However, when allowed to swing, it's the variety of pendulum Foucault used to demonstrate the daily rotation of the earth and incidentally to establish a plane of reference relative to the sun.

The term "plumb," which in carpentry means vertical, comes from the Latin word for lead, *plumbus.* The Romans used lead for pipes (plumbing) as well as for a convenient weight to hang on a string when seeking vertical or assessing the shallowness of water (plumbing the depths).

Habitat: Toolbox of builder, carpenter, or mason. Sold by hardware stores and home centers. The heavy weight, sharp point, and centered string are characteristic.

Primary Use: Finding a vertical line or a point directly above or below a given point. Comparing the stance of posts and walls to a vertical line.

Variations: Old plumb bobs were turned from solid brass; ornate ones may unscrew into several parts. Utilitarian plumb bobs are likely to be six- or eight-sided and shiny. Without a real plumb bob, you could do worse than a citrus reamer tied to a piece of string.

How to Use: 1. **Locate one end of the future vertical line.**

2. **Suspend the plumb bob from that point. When the bob stops swinging its string will be vertical, and its point will be aimed directly at the other end of the vertical line.**

Tool-Kit Minimum: Essential whenever you need to demonstrate which way is up.

76a–c. **PRY BAR**

General Description: *A flat, thick metal bar about as long as your forearm, bent like an elongated L. The bar has beveled ends* with centered notches, plus a teardrop-shaped slot in the long side. It's much too thick and stiff to flex it.

Habitat: Builder's truck and carpenter's toolbox. Sold by hardware stores and home centers.

Primary Uses: In demolition, for pulling nails and prying things apart. In construction, for twisting bowed planks when nailing them in place and levering heavy assemblies into exact position. In repair work, for gently lifting damaged shingles or clapboards so new ones can be slipped into place.

Secondary Uses: Opening windows that were painted shut. Unclogging the snow thrower without sticking your hand down its gullet. Dragging gunk away from clogged drains, also without putting your hand in there. A favorite tool among cat burglars.

Variations: The flat pry bar is similar to the crowbar, with a hexagonal rod of steel with one end bent into a hook; and the cat's paw, a small crowbar for pulling nails and tearing into wooden crates and pallets.

How to Use: 1. **To pull a nail, first assess whether or not the head protrudes above the surface.**

2. **If you can get at the nail head, slip the notch in the short end of the bar underneath it. If the nail head**

**has been set flush or driven under the surface, use the
long end of the bar to dig down to it.**

3. **Press down on the long end of the bar to lever the
nail out of the wood.**

Tool-Kit
Minimum:

Invaluable whenever you want to lift one corner of
the freezer or the grand piano just a smidge.

77.   **SAW, CHOP**

General
Description:

*A round, fat disk mounted on an arm that rises from the
back of a small, metallic platform.* The chop saw is a
complicated piece of apparatus. It has a handle on the
platform and another handle with a trigger inside it
on the fat disk. The platform has a vertical component
(called a "fence") mounted on its back edge. An electrical cord runs into a cylinder the size of a coffee can
mounted off one side. The whole assembly is about
the size of your torso. Fiddling reveals that the fat
disk (called the "blade guard") has several parts; one
of them pivots, exposing a toothy metal disk (a circular saw blade). The blade guard pivots down to the
platform and also slides forward on its arm; the handle on the table can be loosened so the whole thing
rotates. When you pull the trigger in the handle, the
saw blade starts to spin and make a loud noise. Watch
out, as this is a cutting tool and the blade is sharp.

Habitat: Carpenter's truck and woodworking shop. Sold by home centers and tool specialists. The saw blade and platform configuration distinguishes the chop saw from the portable circular saw.

Primary Uses: Cutting wood to length and cutting angles (miters) on the ends of wood. These cuts are necessary in both rough and finish carpentry whenever you want wood and moldings to fit neatly together. Cutting dadoes (grooves across the width of the wood) when making furniture and cabinets.

Operating Principle: The toothy disk is a circular saw blade. Most of the sawing in carpentry and home renovation is crosscutting, that is, cutting the wood to length while leaving a square, tidy end. Since wood is a fibrous material, crosscutting means sawing across the fibers. Sawing in the direction of the fibers, called "ripping," makes the wood narrower in width. Chop saws can crosscut only, they do not rip, nor can they break down sheets of plywood.

Variations: Basic chop saws pivot and miter; the width of wood they can cut is limited by the diameter of the blade. More advanced saws have a sliding arm that increases the width of the cut, plus a tilt mechanism for making a bevel cut. Some also have a laser system to help line up the cut.

Safety Note: Wear your eye protection and hearing protection while operating the chop saw. The disk-shaped housing for the saw blade is a safety guard that, on most saws, completely shrouds the blade until it touches the wood, then it pivots out of the way. It is very important that you do not interfere with the blade guard. The chop saw, inattentively used, can saw fingers clean off your hand.

   Whenever you install or replace the saw blade, be sure to disconnect the electrical power first. You must eliminate any possibility of the saw accidentally becoming switched on while you work inside it.

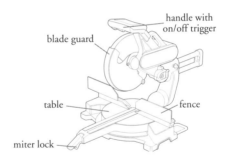

How to Use: 1.   **Study the owner's manual and, with the saw unplugged, experiment with its various settings and movements.**

   2.   **Following the instructions in the owner's manual, set up a scrap length of wood for a test cut. With the saw**

unplugged, be sure you understand where the saw
blade is going to cut and how the guard will move.

3. Before you plug in the saw, be sure its platform is
    clamped or screwed onto the worktable. Also be sure
    the floor around the saw is clear of anything that
    might interfere with footing.

4. Plug in the saw. Place the wood under the saw blade
    and against the saw fence. Hold it there with one
    hand, making sure your hand is safely away from the
    path of the blade.

5. Hold the saw's main handle with your other hand.
    Pull the trigger to switch on the motor and spin the
    saw blade.

6. Check that your holding hand is not in the path of
    the blade. For your safety, acquire the habit of verify-
    ing the position of both hands before any cutting
    operation.

7. Pivot the saw slowly and firmly down into the wood.
    If the saw has a sliding arm, bring it all the way for-
    ward before you lower the blade. Push the blade
    through the wood, then slowly and firmly return it to
    the up position. Release the trigger to shut off the
    motor.

8. **Wait for the blade to coast to a stop. Then release your grip on the wood and the saw handle and remove the cut pieces.**

Tool-Kit
Minimum:

The chop saw makes any home carpentry project quicker, easier, and more accurate.

78. **SAW, PORTABLE CIRCULAR**

General
Description:

A housing about the size of a coffee can mounted on a square metal plate, with a black plastic knob near one edge and an electrical cord. The various components of a portable circular saw include a handle with a trigger and a pivoting housing that protects a toothy metal disk (the saw blade). The housing and plate have a knob controlling the distance between them. There's also an adjustment for tilting the housing relative to the plate. Plugging in the cord and pulling the trigger makes the saw blade rotate, producing a loud noise.

Portability more than makes up for the limited accuracy of the circular saw, and explains why this tool is ubiquitous on carpentry jobs. This virtue becomes a drawback when your mother-in-law spots the saw in the trunk of your car and begins talking about the work she needs done on her rotting deck. Next time, leave your saw at home.

| Habitat: | Carpenter's truck and toolbox. Sold by hardware stores and home centers. Distinguish the circular saw from the table saw by its much smaller size, and from the chop saw by the absence of a fixed base platform. |

| Primary Uses: | Cutting wood to length or width. Cutting large sheets of plywood and wallboard. |

| Variations: | Portable circular saws are manufactured in a variety of sizes with blades ranging between 7 inches (18 cm) and 12 inches (30 cm) in diameter. Some models have a gear drive, which permits deeper cuts. |

| Safety Note: | Wear eye protection, hearing protection, and work boots. Always clamp the wood to be cut onto something solid so you can drive the saw with two hands, and clamp a separate guide piece (called a fence) onto the work so you can steer the saw along it. Learn how the saw's blade guard operates and how to work with it, and do not attempt to defeat it. |

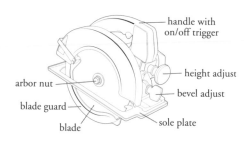

handle with
on/off trigger

height adjust

arbor nut

bevel adjust

blade guard

blade

sole plate

How to Use: 1.   Mark the line to be cut on the wood.

2. Clamp the wood to something solid so that the line of cut is positioned beyond the edge, with nothing under it. Put on your eye and ear protection. Pick up any scraps of wood that might interfere with your footing.

3. Consult the owner's manual and follow its instructions for adjusting the depth of the saw cut. Adjust the depth of cut so that it is larger than the thickness of the wood.

4. With the saw unplugged, position the saw at the start of the cut. Draw a second line on the wood along the edge of the saw base. Clamp a guide piece of wood (a fence) on this line and make sure it is square (see square, page 175).

5. With the saw still unplugged, take a stable stance and rehearse the path of the cut. Make sure you can guide the saw all the way along the edge of the fence. Ensure the saw's cord won't snag and that it does not trail across the line of the cut nor hang underneath it. Some carpenters keep the electrical cord under control by draping it over one shoulder.

6. Plug in the saw and hold it in two hands, one on the trigger handle and the other on the knob. Position

the saw at the start of the cut, tight against the fence, but make sure the saw teeth do not touch the wood.

7. Pull the trigger to start the saw. Some saws have a lever you can lift to retract the blade guard while others retract the guard automatically when you push the saw into the wood.

8. Continue pushing the saw against the fence and along or across the wood until it reaches the other side. Allow the offcut to fall to the floor while you concentrate on lifting the saw off the wood, releasing the trigger, and waiting for the blade to stop.

9. Put the saw down on the worktable or floor before you reach for the cut piece.

10. If you need to stop partway through the cut, release the trigger and wait for the blade to stop before proceeding.

Tool-Kit Minimum: A portable circular saw is invaluable when cutting wood.

79. SAW, PORTABLE RECIPROCATING

General Description: *A plastic and metal apparatus about as long and thick as your lower leg with a D-shaped handle at one end, a fist-sized clamping device at the other, and a bayonet-style saw blade projecting from the clamp.* The stiff blade is about as long as your wide-spread hand, with small saw teeth when compared to circular saws. A power cord emerges from the handle, which has a trigger inside it. When you plug in the cord and squeeze the trigger, the saw emits a loud vibrating noise and the blade and clamp assembly pumps aggressively to and fro.

Habitat: Builder's truck. Sold by home centers and tool specialists. Many portable power tools are similar: Make tentative identification, whether or not the saw blade is present, by checking the clamping device. If it has a slot to accept flat blades, it's a reciprocating saw; if it has a round opening, it's probably a drill.

Primary Use: Essential for demolishing walls, floors, furniture, plumbing, houses, or cars.

Variations: Reciprocating saws can be fit with blades for cutting wood, masonry, or metal.

How to Use: 1. **Choose a saw blade whose teeth match the primary material you wish to demolish. Mount it in the blade clamp according to the owner's manual.**

2. **Wear eye protection, hearing protection, workboots, and gloves.**

3. Think about whether there is live electrical wiring inside the demolition target (see outlet tester, page 119). If so, make sure the electricity has been powered off at the main panel. Think also about whether there might be pipes containing water inside the target. If so, find the main shut-off valve and shut it off.

4. Plan your attack: Usually it's best to start at one edge of the target.

5. Take a stable stance. Brace the nose of the saw against the target with the saw teeth facing it. Pull the trigger, then pivot the saw on its nose so the blade encounters the target.

6. Maneuver the saw so its nose remains braced while the blade pistons back and forth.

7. Steer the saw through the target. You'll feel it catch on nails and other hardware, but usually you can bull right through. If the target is metal, such as a fat pipe, lubricate the cut with a light oil intended for metal cutting.

8. Alternate sawing with pounding and prying until the target has been demolished.

Tool-Kit Minimum: If you had to face down the Terminator, the reciprocating saw might give you a chance.

80. 📷 **SAWHORSE**

General
Description:

Two inverted V shapes made of thick wood, connected by a stout plank, that stand about thigh high. A sawhorse's name comes from its distinctive shape—the two sets of legs mimic those of an equine—and "horse" or "trestle" is generally used to describe freestanding, four-legged structures used in building, masonry, general repair work, and gymnastics. Cross bracing holds the legs of the horse in place, making the structure stiff and sturdy.

Habitat:

Job site and workshop. Sold in plastic versions at home centers. Sawhorses work best in pairs, so when you have identified one, look for another nearby.

Primary
Use:

Portable support for work in progress, especially for sawing.

Secondary
Uses:

To paint a paneled door, unhinge it and lay it flat across sawhorses. When unexpected guests arrive, create a sturdy but temporary table using sawhorses for supports.

Operating
Principle:

A three-sided construction (the braced V shape) is inherently rigid and stable.

How to Use: 1. **Choose (or make) a pair of horses whose height is appropriate.**

2. **Separate the horses so the distance between them is less than the length of the material to be supported.**

3. **Lift the workpiece and set it across the sawhorses with overhang.**

81a–c. **SCISSORS**

General
Description:

Two flat bars of metal crossed in an X shape and connected with a pivot, with sharp points and edges at one end and loop-shaped openings at the other. The openings fit the thumb and fingers, allowing the opposable thumb to operate the metal bars, opening and closing the X and making a snicking sound. The handles stop against one another, but the long sharp edges pass by. If you put a piece of paper between the sharp edges and work the handles, it immediately becomes two pieces of paper, both smaller.

Habitat:

Almost anywhere. Sold by hardware stores, hobby shops, and supermarkets. Separate scissors from other X-shaped metal tools such as tile nippers, loppers, wire cutters, and pliers by their long, sharp bypass blades and asymmetric shape: one blade can be set flush to a table while the other pivots during cutting.

Primary
Use:

Cutting large pieces of paper and fabric into smaller ones. Cutting tape, ribbon, or string.

Operating Principle:	The pivoting action makes the sharp blades slide past one another in an efficient slicing cut, exerting enormous force on their tiny but ever-advancing intersection with the workpiece.
Variations:	Scissors come in right-handed or left-handed models.

How to Use: 1. **Make a cutting line with chalk or pencil.**

2. **Hold the scissors and open their blades. Set the start of the line between the blades.**

3. **Close the handles together so the blades slice along the line.**

4. **Open the handles, reposition the scissors on the line, and repeat as necessary.**

Note: **To start a hole, pinch a fold in the material and snip it with the tips of the scissors. To rough cut a length of cloth, hold the scissors low to the table and slightly parted. Pull the cloth tight with your other hand as you push the scissors forward to slice the material.**

82a–g. 📷 **SCREWDRIVERS**

General Description: *A plastic handle with a metal cylinder sticking straight out of it.* The end of the metal actually is a precisely shaped tip, sometimes flat, sometimes cross shaped or star shaped, and sometimes square, to fit the sockets in the heads of common varieties of screws. The handle has grooves and corners that make it easy to take a firm grip.

Habitat: Every toolbox. Widely sold. The grippable handle, straight blade, and precise, not-sharp tip distinguishes the screwdriver from otherwise similar sharp-pointed awls and sharp-edged chisels.

Primary Use: Driving screws. Removing screws.

Operating Principle: The wheel. The handle is fatter than the tip, so turning the handle with moderate force transmits large force to the relatively small tip; moderately tilting the handle increases the leverage, which is why long screwdrivers work better than stubby ones.

Variations: Straight tips fit screws with slotted heads. Cross-shaped tips are for cross-head (Phillips-type) screws. Square tips nestle into square-drive (Robertson) screws. Star-shaped tips fit automotive and electronic Torx screws. Each type comes in numerous sizes. Some screwdrivers have interchangeable tips, which also can be chucked in electric and hand-powered drills (page 199). The Yankee screwdriver has a spiral shank with a ratchet that converts your hard push into rotation. At the bar, the screwdriver is made by pouring vodka and orange juice over ice.

How to Use: 1. **Choose a screwdriver whose tip matches the screw.**

2. **Mark the location of the screw hole and use the center punch (page 278) or awl (page 186) to make a dimple there.**

3. **Plant the screw on the mark and engage the screwdriver in its head.**

4. **Push and turn the screwdriver handle. One direction will drive the screw, the other will remove it.**

Tool-Kit Minimum: Two straight and two cross-head drivers will handle most household screwing.

83a–c. **SQUARE**

General Description: *A flat, metal L shape with arms about as long as your forearms.* Squares defy their name by not actually being shaped like a square; instead they represent two sides and one corner of a square. They have numbered markings along the edges, plus tables of numbers on the flat surfaces. The shorter, fatter arm is the tongue. The longer, thinner arm is the blade.

Habitat:	Toolbox of builder, carpenter, mason, or artist. Sold by hardware stores and home centers. The two arms meeting at a right angle is characteristic; squarelike tools with a pivot instead of a rigid corner are bevel gauges.
Primary Use:	Marking square corners and checking corners for squareness.
Secondary Uses:	Marking miters and bevels. Guiding the circular saw for square crosscutting. Adepts use the square to lay out and cut the carriage that supports perfectly spaced stairs, a high point of the building arts.
Operating Principle:	Squareness is not arbitrary—a corner is square or it isn't. Square is a right angle, 90 degrees, a quarter of a circle. Square corners fill two- and three-dimensional space without any gaps. This property makes squareness more useful than other shapes.
Variations:	The speed square is triangular with a flange along one edge. The try square has one wooden arm and one metal one. Drywall squares have a 4-foot tongue. Wood- and metal-workers favor a combination square, whose head slides along a steel rule.
Safety Note:	Carpenters so highly value a truly square square that borrowing, misplacing, or dropping one places the miscreant at immediate risk of bodily harm. Be

extremely careful whenever you are using a square that belongs to someone else.

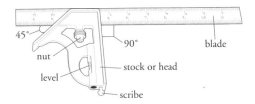

How to Use:

1. **To lay out a square end on a piece of wood, measure to locate the future corner and make a mark there.**

2. **Lay the square flat on the wood with its tongue tight against the edge of the wood. Tilt it to make it catch.**

3. **Move the square along the wood until its blade coincides with the mark.**

4. **Draw a line along the blade.**

5. **To assess the squareness of an existing corner, fit the square into it or around it. Press the tongue tight against one side of the corner under investigation.**

6. **Examine the relationship between the square's blade and the other side of the corner. If they coincide, the corner is square. If not, it's not.**

Note: **Once in a while the truth of the square itself comes into question. To assess it, mark a line across a straight piece of wood as in Steps 1 through 4. Then flip the square over so its tongue points the other way, and mark another line. If the two lines coincide, the square is square. If they diverge, the square is off.**

Tool-Kit Minimum: The triangular speed square is less versatile but easier to use than the L-shaped framing square.

---

84. [📷]   **STUD FINDER**

General Description: *A plastic block about the size of a cell phone with a row of light-emitting diodes on the face and a single push-button.* Close inspection of a stud finder reveals a battery compartment. Pressing the button makes the diodes flash green and red.

Habitat: Handy homeowner's tool kit. Sold by hardware stores and home centers.

Primary Use: Locating solid support inside walls, before driving nails or screws into the wall in order to attach something.

Secondary Uses: Not useful for finding studs in social situations, unless the criterion for studhood is being able to identify the stud finder itself.

Operating Principle:	A low-power electromagnetic field changes when it intersects with wood masses and with metal; the stud finder detects the change and displays it in flashing diodes.

How to Use: 1. **Place the stud finder flat on the wall, row of lights pointing up and down.**

2. **Hold the button, move the finder from side to side across the wall, and observe the lights.**

3. **When the lights begin to flash or change, you've found something. Mark it with a pencil.**

Note: **Wall studs are always vertical, and in modern construction, 16 inches (40 cm) apart center to center. Find one and you've found them all.**

85a–c. **TAPE MEASURE**

General Description: *A square, palm-sized case with a belt clip on one side and a slide or toggle on one edge.* Close inspection reveals a little metal tab protruding from one corner of the case. When you pull on the tab, you find that it's on the end of a thin, spring-loaded metal tongue that's easy to pull out of the case; when you let go it snaps back inside. Fiddling with the toggle locks the tongue in the extended position.

The retractable metal tongue, or blade, is painted yellow with black hatch marks and numbers all along it. The numbers on tapes sold in the United States indicate inches, while those made for sale everywhere else in the world indicate centimeters. The last joint on your little finger is about an inch long, and its nail is about a centimeter wide.

Inches and feet (that is, 12 inches), although the most common measuring system among American handypersons and the principal set of markings on a U.S. tape measure, coexist alongside another system known as the on-center distance between studs, generally agreed as 16 inches (40 cm) and marked in red on most tape measures. Studs standing 16 inches (40 cm) apart might seem a good recipe for girls' night out, but the term refers to the distance between vertical 2x4s, called "studs," that form a wall's skeleton.

Habitat:	Apron or tool belt of most handypersons; also found in junk drawers nationwide. Sold by hardware stores and home centers. The case with the retracting tongue is sufficient for identification.
Primary Use:	Measuring objects and distances between objects.
Secondary Uses:	Measuring the depth of holes. Finding the midpoint between two points.

Operating
Principle:

There was a time when your inch was not necessarily the size of mine, causing much argument. Avoiding disagreements required the creation of reference standards people could use to calibrate measuring tools; the standard for inches is kept near Washington, D.C., while the one for centimeters lives near Paris.

Variations:

Builders use a 100-foot (30 m) measuring tape to lay out walls and foundations. Tailors and seamstresses use a flexible cloth tape (conforms easily to the curves of the body) that they keep in a coil (or a tangle), not in a metal case.

How to Use:

1. **It's not always easy to isolate the distance you need to measure from adjacent distances you could measure but don't really need to know. Begin by clarifying what is to be measured.**

2. **Catch one side of the distance to be measured with the metal hook on the tape measure.**

3. **Pull the case to extend the tape until it crosses the other side of the distance in question.**

4. **Read and record the distance printed on the tape. You might have to interpolate between whole numbers. The little hatch marks indicate subdivisions into halves, quarters, eighths, sixteenths, and thirty-seconds of an inch. A millimeter, or one-tenth of a centimeter,**

falls about halfway between a sixteenth of an inch
and a thirty-second of an inch.

Tool-Kit
Minimum:

A 25-foot (7.5 m) tape in a bright-colored, easy-to-
find case is indispensible.

86. 📷 **TIE-DOWN STRAPS**

General
Description:

Flat fabric ribbons several times as long as you are,
woven from tough nylon with a metal buckle on one
end. No mere plain piece of string, tie-down straps
have a sturdy buckle that locks and releases by way of
a spring-loaded tab.

Habitat:

Trunk of car or back of pickup truck. Sold by hardware stores and canoe liveries.

Primary
Uses:

Fastening your load of lumber and plywood onto the
car's roof rack. Strapping your canoe onto the roof
rack. Anchoring furniture inside moving vans.

Variations:

You can do the same job with rope, provided you
know how to tie knots that won't slip.

How to Use: 1.

Always use two straps to secure a load. Choose sturdy
straps with buckles designed for anchoring loads.

2.

Place the load on the roof rack and center it.

3. **Loop the tie-down straps under the roof rack.**

4. **Drape both ends across the top of the load.**

5. **Feed one free end of the strap under the roof rack on the other side of the load.**

6. **Feed the free end of the strap into the one-way buckle and tighten it firmly.**

7. **Tuck the loose end of the strap under the load, or catch it inside the car door.**

Tool-Kit
Minimum:
A car with a roof rack and a pair of tie-down straps will get you and your stuff safely home.

87. **UTILITY KNIFE**

General
Description:
A metal handle about as long as your hand and as thick as your thumb, with a shiny triangle-shaped blade protruding from one end. A utility knife's blade is sharp along one edge. A sliding tab on the knife handle, when pressed and slid, moves the blade in and out of the handle. Continued investigation finds a fat screw in the side of the handle. When the screw is removed, the handle comes apart. The triangular blade turns out to be one end of a finger-length double-ended knife. Notches on one edge click onto the extending

tab. There's also a spare blade in a compartment inside the handle.

Utility knives are remarkably easy to misplace, especially when moving. Get a new one for everyone involved in the move.

Habitat: Any toolbox or junk drawer. Sold by hardware stores and home centers.

Primary Use: Cutting flat building materials such as drywall, wallboard, shingles, vapor barrier, insulation, or carpet. Opening boxes or cutting packaging and strapping off products. Trimming parts to fit.

Variations: Special blades help cut diverse materials such as carpet and acrylic plastic. Some knives have mechanisms for changing blades without disassembling the handle.

How to Use: 1. **Hold the knife in your fist with your thumb on top of the handle just behind the dull edge of the blade.**

• **To cut wallboard, score the line on one side while holding the utility knife against a metal straight-edge. Snap the wallboard away from the cut, then run the knife in the fold along the back side.**

• **To cut vapor barriers and building papers, first staple in place, then trim the excess by drawing the knife across it.**

- To cut carpet, make the layout line and the cut on the back side.

- To cut asphalt tile, score one side with the knife then snap the tile away from the score, just as you would for glass (see glass cutter, page 40).

- To cut an acrylic sheet, fit a special hook-shaped blade in the knife and make repeated passes on the line. Some acrylics need to be scored on both sides.

2. Replace the blade as soon as it gets dull.

Tool-Kit Minimum: Easier to use than a box cutter, a utility knife is an indispensable addition to any junk drawer.

VII. Woodworking

Woodworking picks up where carpentry leaves off, focusing on interior finishing and detailing, cabinets, and furniture. More precise than carpentry, woodworking gives you the ability to create and trim parts that fit, providing you with attractive, useful, and comfortable results.

88a–d. 📷

AWL

General
Description:

A pointed metal cylinder about as long as a finger sticking straight out of a stubby handle. The point on the metal is quite sharp. A metal button is set into the top of the handle.

Habitat:

Toolbox of woodworker and builder. Sold by hardware stores and home centers. Distinguish the awl from the similar screwdriver by its sharp point.

Primary
Uses:

Poking a tiny shallow hole for starting screws and nails. Making a pinprick to record a measurement or location. When used with a square, scratching a layout line.

Secondary
Uses:

Anchoring the plumb bob, chalk line, or long tape measure.

Variations: The gimlet is an awl whose tip has sharp threads like a wood screw, used for making larger holes; some gimlets have T handles.

How to Use: 1. **When you are hanging a picture or a shelf, measure or use your stud finder (page 178) to locate the first hole for a nail or screw.**

2. **Set the point of the awl on that location.**

3. **Hold the shank of the awl in one hand, and with the palm of the other push the awl into the wall slightly.**

4. **On hard materials such as wood, punch the awl with your palm or tap with a hammer.**

5. **Pull the awl from the hole and replace it with the tip of a nail or screw.**

6. **Drive the nail or screw.**

Tool-Kit Minimum: One awl is all you need; awl you really need is love.

89.   **BEVEL GAUGE**

General Description: *A wooden handle (called the "stock") with a flat metal blade (called the "tongue") protruding from a narrow slot in one end.* The tongue has one round end and one end cut at an angle, with a wide slot cut in its face and another slot in the side of the stock. A turn screw on the stock clamps the two parts together at the pivot point. When you loosen the turn screw, you can rotate the metal tongue to make various angles with the stock, and you can slide the tongue via its slot so the tool's overall shape varies between an L and a T.

Habitat: Woodworker's bench, builder's toolbox. Sold by hardware stores, home centers, and woodworking specialty shops. The pivot between stock and tongue is definitive; squares have a fixed 90-degree angle between tongue and stock.

Primary Use: Recording and transferring angles from one place to another, usually so one part (such as a molding or a chair seat) can be cut to a neat fit into a corner or an opening. The accurate transfer of angles is essential when making dovetail joints in wood.

Secondary Uses: To measure angles, use the bevel gauge to transfer them to a protractor, a flat semicircle of metal or plastic divided into 180 equal sections, called "degrees."

Variations: Machinist's protractors have a pivoting tongue that allows them not only to be used like bevel gauges, but also to directly measure angles in degrees. Uniformly dividing a circle with 180 diameters creates 360 degrees; 90 degrees or a quarter circle defines a right angle.

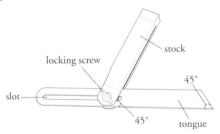

How to Use: 1. **Locate the corner, intersection, or vertex of the angle you wish to record.**

2. **Loosen the thumbscrew on the bevel gauge and slide the blade so that you can press the stock against one side of the angle and the tongue against the other.**

3. **Hold the stock and blade in place on the angle while you tighten the thumbscrew. This records the angle.**

4. **Carry the bevel gauge to the part you wish to fit. Set the stock against one edge and transfer the angle by drawing a line along the tongue.**

Tool-Kit Minimum: Surprisingly handy when installing crown moldings or working with the off-kilter spaces in old houses.

90a–c. 📷   **CALIPER**

General
Description:
Two identically curved pieces of flat metal, each about as long as your hand, joined at one end with a pivot. A screw protrudes from one side, and when you turn it the opening between the metal pieces changes. If you close the calipers completely, the ends of the two arms meet together. A spring works against the screw so the apparatus stays tight.

Habitat:
Toolbox of woodworker, builder, and mechanic. Sold by hardware stores and home centers. The similar compass (page 196) has straight arms, one of them ending in a pencil holder, whereas calipers are curvy.

Primary
Use:
Measuring and transferring thicknesses, inside dimensions, and distances from parts and places inaccessible to the tape measure or ruler. A suitable caliper can tell you the diameter of a dowel or drill bit as well as the thickness in the center of a plate.

Operating
Principle:
Local space is not subject to relativity, so a dimension recorded over here remains the same when transferred over there. This would not be true inside a spaceship traveling near the speed of light.

Variations:
The micrometer caliper is shaped like the letter P, with a precise arrangement of threaded collars with markings that report the distance measured in thou-

sandths of an inch. The vernier caliper does the same trick using a linear scale. The dial caliper reports the measurement via a needle set in a circular dial.

How to Use: 1. **Choose a caliper whose jaws open far enough to fit the object being calipered.**

2. **Turn the screw to open the jaws wider than the workpiece.**

3. **Set the caliper on the workpiece and tighten the screw so both jaws make contact.**

4. **Without changing the setting, slide the caliper off the workpiece.**

5. **Hold the caliper up to a tape measure (page 179) or square (page 175) and read the transferred dimension. This step is not necessary with dial calipers and micrometers because they directly report the measurement.**

Tool-Kit Minimum: A plastic dial caliper from the hardware store is both affordable and surprisingly accurate.

91a–e. **CARVING TOOLS**

General Description: *Shiny metal blades with shaped, extremely sharp tips protruding straight out from wooden handles.* Carving tools look like screwdrivers except for their carefully shaped and very sharp cutting edges.

Carving tools come in hundreds of sizes and styles with such interesting names as gouge (a scooped edge), sweep (a shallow gouge), skew (a straight edge set at an angle), fluter (a deep gouge), veiner (a reverse gouge for shaping a ridge of wood), V-tool (shaped like its name), macaroni (makes a square-bottomed channel), fluteroni (makes a deep U-shaped channel with rounded corners). Some flare to a wide, fishtail shape, some have a bent shank, and some have a back bend in the shank.

Habitat:
Woodworker's bench or artist's toolbox. Sold by specialty tool dealers. Often found in a canvas roll with similar tools and a mallet.

Primary Use:
Carving wood into such interesting shapes as oak leaves, regimental crests, grizzly bears, human portraits, and signs.

Operating Principle:
If you want to cut into a piece of wood and leave a particular shape behind, you need a sharp tool of approximately the same shape. Carving tools that are not sharp will crush the wood instead of cutting it.

Variations:
Engraving tools are small carving tools with fat little handles; they're always driven by hand pressure, not with a mallet.

How to Use: 1. **Choose a carving tool whose shape you like.**

2. **With a pen or pencil, draw the shape you wish to carve on the workpiece.**

3. **Hold the carving gouge like a dagger, your fist loosely wrapped around the handle and your thumb near the end, not near the blade.**

4. **Position the sharp end of the tool against the wood to be removed.**

5. **Use a mallet (page 211) to tap the sharp end of the gouge into the wood. A shallow angle works best.**

6. **Lever the handle to lift the chip out of the workpiece. You might have to make more than one cut before the chip breaks free.**

7. **In general, carve downhill with respect to grain direction (see chisel, page 194, for a discussion).**

8. **Repeat until the shape you had in mind emerges from the wood.**

Tool-Kit Minimum: Not hard to learn to use, but it takes a lifetime to become an adept wood-carver.

92a–c. **CHISEL**

General
Description:

A shiny metal blade with a straight, sharp end projecting from a hand-sized wooden or plastic handle. The metal blade is very flat on one side, while the other side has a beveled end. The two adjacent sides are beveled as well. Wood-handled chisels have a metal ring around the handle where the blade enters; this helps keep the handle from splitting. Some chisels have a tight iron ring around the top end of the wooden handle.

Habitat:

Woodworker's bench or builder's toolbox. Sold by hardware stores and home centers, often in graduated sets of six or eight. The flat back and sharp end distinguish chisels from otherwise similar carving tools, which are neither flat nor straight.

Primary
Use:

Removing wood in a controlled way to make two pieces of wood fit together, as when making a square opening, tidying a joint, or beveling a corner.

Operating
Principle:

The chisel's flat side (called its "face") makes it a self-jigging tool. This means that once you begin, the cut guides the chisel's continuing progress. Wood is made of fibers, which affect how the piece of wood can be cut. You can see the fibers and determine their direction with the naked eye. Cutting against the grain causes splintering and splitting; cutting across the grain leaves a rough surface.

Variations: Chisels are made in a large range of widths and lengths to match various jobs. They also have different handle styles. Chisels designed for excavating deep holes in wood have a stout shoulder (or bolster) where the blade meets the handle. Chisels designed for paring in the middle of flat surfaces have a cranked shank so the handle doesn't interfere with the work. Very large chisels, called "slicks," are used in boat-building and timber frame carpentry. Japanese chisels are called "*nomi*."

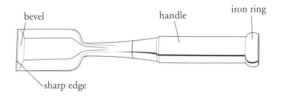

How to Use: 1. **Choose a chisel whose blade looks the right size for the job at hand.**

2. **Use a pencil to mark the wood.**

3. **Chisels make two kinds of cuts, chopping and paring. Chopping cuts require holding the chisel like a dagger, thumb on its handle end, while paring cuts go better if you grip the chisel like a spatula, thumb on top of the handle near the blade. Either cut can be powered by the unaided hand, or by a hammer (page 149) or mallet (page 211).**

4. **Cut into the wood, removing it in thin slices.**

Tool-Kit
Minimum:
A 1 1/2-inch (3.5 cm) chisel with a short blade (called a "stubby") will help set most of the hinges and pare most of the edges a homeowner is likely to encounter.

93. **COMPASS**

General
Description:
Two thin pieces of metal connected with a pivot, making a V shape. One of the metal lengths ends in a sharp point, while the other carries a pencil. A threaded rod with a dime-sized nut on it connects the two arms near the pivot; turning the nut changes the span of the V. The whole thing is not as long as an adult hand.

Habitat:
Toolbox of builder and woodworker. Sold by hardware and art supply stores.

Primary
Uses:
Drawing circles and arcs. Uniformly dividing lines, bisecting angles, and drawing such shapes as triangles, pentagons, hexagons, and octagons. If you replace its pencil point with a small knife blade, the compass can cut circles out of sheet materials such as paper, foil, vinyl, and fabric.

Operating
Principle:
Any circle is a collection of points, each the same distance from a single center point. This relationship is enforced by the construction of the compass.

Variations: Dividers look like compasses but have two sharp metal points. Calipers have two curved arms that meet when fully closed. Two points called "trammels," when mounted on a yardstick, can operate as a very large compass.

How to Use: 1. **Choose a compass that is large enough for the circle or arc you intend to draw.**

2. **With a combination square or tape measure, adjust the compass opening to match the radius (that is, the distance from center to edge) of the future circle.**

3. **Set the sharp point on the center of the circle and, without changing the compass setting, drag the pencil point all the way around.**

Tool-Kit Minimum: Once you get around to buying a compass, you'll wonder how you ever managed without it.

94. **COPING SAW**

General Description: *A metal frame about as long and wide as an adult's hand, with an extremely narrow saw blade on one side and a straight handle in line with the blade.* The saw blade is very small. A pin on each end of the blade fits into slots in the frame. Twisting the handle tightens and loosens the blade. Twisting the handle also allows the blade to be turned to almost any angle, which allows the saw to make deeper cuts and to reach far into workpieces.

If you wanted to reproduce a jigsaw puzzle, this is the handsaw you would need. Depending on the way the saw is mounted, the saw cuts on the pull or on the push stroke. Set it according to personal preference; it doesn't matter to the workpiece.

Coping blades are more likely to break before they become dull; they can't be resharpened and so must be replaced.

Habitat:	Toolbox of woodworker and finish carpenter. Sold by hardware stores and home centers. Although the coping saw superficially resembles a hacksaw (page 286), it's both shorter and deeper.
Primary Uses:	Making intricate cuts in thin metal and plastic. Sawing one end of a molding so it fits over the profile of an adjacent molding to make a neat and tight inside corner; this is called a "cope cut" (hence the name of the saw). Sawing waste wood from dovetail joints. When equipped with a jeweler's blade, sawing thin metal and other hard materials such as mother-of-pearl for inlays.
Operating Principle:	The coping saw's blade-mounting system permits making extremely tight turns. It also allows the blade to be fed through a hole, for cutting an inside shape.

Variations: The fretsaw is similar but has a very deep frame. The jigsaw is the equivalent powered saw; it has a horizontal worktable and an up-and-down blade mechanism. Jeweler's saws use blades that are even finer than coping saw blades.

How to Use: 1. **Make a layout line on the work and clamp it upright in a vise or flat on a workbench with the layout extending beyond the support.**

2. **Grip the handle with both hands for steadiness and control. Orient the saw blade square to the surface.**

3. **Make light, short strokes to start the saw. In delicate materials, continue sawing the same way; in solid wood, extend the stroke to the full length of the saw blade.**

4. **Steer the saw around corners while advancing the cut. To make a sharp corner, approach from both sides.**

Tool-Kit Minimum: One regular coping saw with an assortment of blades.

---

95. 📷 **HAND DRILL**

General Description: *An eggbeater-like device with one large handle on top, a small knob on a crank attached to the gears, and another knob attached to its main shank.* The hand drill is about as long as an adult's forearm. A socket or chuck sits opposite the top handle, knurled as if it had been imprinted with coarse cloth. When you turn the knurled chuck, its opening size changes. When you turn the gear, the chuck also goes around. The top handle has an oversized cap that screws off like a jar lid, and there are drill bits inside.

Habitat: Toolbox of a woodworker. Sold by hardware stores and home centers. The eggbeater is the only other thing that looks remotely like a hand drill.

Primary Use: Drilling small holes in wood, metal, leather, and plastic. Before there were electrical drills, the hand drill was the tool of choice for small holes. It's extremely precise and controllable, often preferred over power drills by artisans who make jewelry and other delicate objects.

Secondary Uses: Twisting cord to make trim for upholstery projects. When fit with a paddle or eggbeater attachment from an electric mixer, stirring paint.

Variations: A larger version of the hand drill has a curved plate in place of the top handle and a two-speed gearshift. The curved plate fits against the operator's chest, providing lots of pressure with both hands free for guidance when drilling small and medium-sized holes in metal.

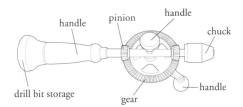

How to Use: 1. Choose a drill bit (page 146) whose size matches the future hole. You can measure the size with a caliper (page 190).

2. Insert the drill bit in the chuck and tighten it.

3. Mark the location of the future hole.

4. Set the point of the drill bit on the mark and aim the hand drill in the direction you want the hole to go, usually straight up and down (square to the surface).

5. Hold the top handle in one hand and the crank handle in the other. Maintain light pressure on the top handle while you turn the crank handle. One direction advances the drill bit while the other retracts it.

6. Note how deep the drill bit has gone and stop when the hole is deep enough. You might need to retract the bit to clear the debris, which otherwise would clog the action.

Tool-Kit
Minimum:

Every tool kit needs one, not only for times when there is no electricity, but also when the hole has to be accurate and neat, with minimum risk of damage to the workpiece.

96a–c. 📷 **HANDSAW**

General
Description:

A thin steel plate, long and tapered like the silhouette of your leg from ankle to knee, with sharp teeth cut into one long edge and a handle mounted on the wider end. In Shakespeare's play *Hamlet*, the title character says, "I am but mad north-north-west: when the wind is southerly I know a hawk from a handsaw." Interpreted through the eyes of a handyman, Hamlet's handsaw would have been a lot like a modern toolbox saw; *hawk* or *hok* is the Middle English name for a square board used to carry mortar and plaster from mixing tub to work site.

Modern saws feature handles made of wood or plastic. The open part of the handle tilts toward the top side of the blade, matching the tilt of your palm with respect to your forearm. This matters because working the saw means pumping it back and forth until its teeth have chewed all the way through the workpiece.

Wood is made of long fibers that all run in the same direction, held together by a compound called "lignin." When cutting with the grain, along the length of the fibers, the blade can easily slip between. When cutting across the grain, perpendicular to the length, the saw must sever each individual fiber. Sawing along the length, called "ripping," is different from sawing across the width, called "crosscutting."

Handsaws are manufactured with two different kinds of teeth, one for crosscutting and the other for ripping. You can tell the difference by looking closely at their spacing and tip shape. Saw teeth for crosscutting are small, closely spaced (between 8 and 15 to the inch, or 3 to 6 per cm), and rise to sharp points like knives. Saw teeth for ripping are relatively wide (between 4 and 8 to the inch, or 1 1/2 to 3 per cm) and rise to straight-across points like little chisels.

Because you can buy lumber already ripped to convenient widths, most of the sawing done when making furniture is crosscutting, and general-purpose handsaws usually have crosscut teeth. Make angled cuts and saw plywood—which consists of thin layers of wood with alternating grain—with a crosscut saw.

Habitat: Woodworker's bench and toolbox or builder's truck. Sold by hardware stores, home centers, and woodworking tool specialists.

Primary Uses: Cutting a piece of wood the desired size and shape. Cutting plywood, wallboard, or fiberboard.

Secondary
Uses:

Jug bands make music on old handsaws. To lay down the rhythm, flex the blade back and forth while tapping your thumb on the metal. To make a melody, bend the sawblade and stroke it with a horsehair bow or a fine file, like a violin.

Operating
Principle:

Each of the saw's sharp little teeth cuts a tiny distance into the wood, with the combined action of all the teeth creating a blade-wide slot, called the "kerf." The technical term for the sawdust that comes out of the kerf is "swarf." Western saws cut on the push stroke, while Japanese saws cut on the pull stroke. Both kinds of saw are designed so their return stroke clears the swarf without advancing the cut.

Variations:

Micro saws for hobby work have blades the length of your hand, with teeth almost too small to distinguish. Old-fashioned felling saws and ripping saws are man high with teeth as long and broad as your thumb. The backsaw, gent's saw, and dovetail saw, for making fine joints in hardwood, have a heavy ridge of metal on the edge opposite their teeth for both stiffness and balance. Flooring saws have a curved nose for starting a cut in the middle of a piece of wood. Japanese saws have a straight handle rather than the D handle common on Western saws, with longer teeth. Japanese ryoba-style saws cut both ways, with crosscutting teeth on one edge and ripping teeth on the other.

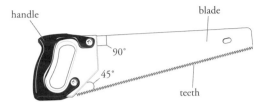

How to Use: 1. **Choose a crosscut saw or a ripsaw according to the grain direction of the wood you want to cut. For plywood, choose a crosscut saw.**

2. **Draw a cut line on the workpiece.**

3. **Place the workpiece on a worktable or across sawhorses (page 171) so that the line of the cut extends beyond the supporting surface. Clamp the wood so it won't move.**

4. **Grip the saw in your dominant hand, teeth pointing down, and take a comfortable marching stance. Plant the teeth on the far edge of the wood, on or right next to the line. Align your arm and shoulder with the cut.**

5. **To start the saw, steady the blade with your thumb while you make short little strokes using just the weight of the blade.**

6. Once the saw has entered the wood, move your steadying hand safely away from the action; otherwise the saw might jump out of its kerf and cut you. Lengthen your sawing stroke. Work the saw back and forth from your shoulder with smooth and steady pushes, applying only a small amount of pressure.

7. At the end of the cut, support and catch the falling wood with your holding hand. If it drops, the wood is likely to splinter.

Note: It's very difficult to correct a saw cut once it starts to veer off the line. Instead, turn the workpiece around and restart from the other edge.

Tool-Kit Minimum: A 15-inch (38 cm) toolbox saw with 8 to 12 teeth per inch (3 to 5 per cm).

---

97. **JIGSAW**

General Description: *A squarish block of plastic and metal about the size of a fat hardcover novel, with a short saw blade sticking out near one corner.* A hand-sized hole with a trigger is set in the middle of the tool and an electrical cord emerges from one side. The blade protrudes through a smooth metal sole plate that's smaller than an adult hand. If you plug the cord into an electrical outlet and squeeze the trigger, the mechanism makes rhythmic grating noises, and the blade churns up and down.

The portable jigsaw (also called a "saber saw") is an extremely versatile powered saw. With the right blade, it can cut most everyday materials. Unlike other power saws, a jigsaw isn't capable of causing grievous bodily harm. It can be guided freehand, steered along a straight edge, or, for cutting circles, tethered to a center point. Versatility has a price: It's difficult to keep a jigsaw cutting straight, and it does not leave a smooth surface behind.

The jigsaw's smooth sole plate, the base of the tool, has a number of mechanisms associated with it, including a slot with a locking screw where blades may be inserted, a tilt and tilt-lock screw, and (on recent saws) a blade advance control. Some jigsaws have a variable speed control.

Habitat: Woodworking shop, builder's truck, or handyman's toolbox. Sold by hardware stores and home centers. In the workshop, there's probably a short saw blade sticking out of the sole plate. In the store, blades will be sold nearby but not mounted in the saw.

Primary Use: Making straight and curved saw cuts in wood, metal, and plastic. If you want to make a plywood Santa, the jigsaw's what you need.

Secondary Use: Starting and cutting a hole in the middle of a plywood or wallboard panel.

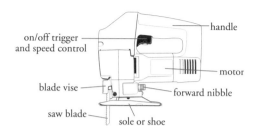

on/off trigger
and speed control

handle

blade vise

motor

saw blade

forward nibble

sole or shoe

How to Use: 1. **Choose a jigsaw blade that's meant for the material you intend to cut (consult the blade packaging). Unplug the saw's electrical cord and then install the blade according to your owner's manual, with its teeth pointing forward and down. Put on your safety glasses.**

2. **Place the workpiece on sawhorses (page 171) or a worktable, with the line to be cut overhanging the edge of the support.**

3. **Plug in the saw. Control the cord by draping it over your shoulder to avoid sawing it.**

4. **Set the front edge of the sole plate on the workpiece with the saw blade on the line.**

5. **Squeeze the trigger to start the saw. Press the sole plate down on the workpiece and steer the saw forward along the layout line. Release the trigger to stop**

the saw to brush away the sawdust or assess your progress.

6.   Allow the saw to cut at its own pace. If you force it or exert any sideways pressure, it will wander away from the layout line.

7.   Keep the saw moving forward while steering around curves and corners. To make a tight corner, saw into it from one direction and release the trigger so you can lift the stopped saw out of the work. Then saw into the corner from the other direction.

Note: To jigsaw a straight line, use a straight piece of wood as a guide fence. Measure the distance from the saw blade to the edge of its sole plate. Clamp the guide fence this distance from the layout line. Test the setup in scrap wood.

Tool-Kit Minimum: Because it is so safe and versatile, a jigsaw is the first powered saw to acquire.

---

98.   **MAGNIFYING GLASS**

General Description: *A glass disk mounted in a ring with a handle.* The glass is not flat but thicker in the middle than at the edges, and when you look at the world through it, the scene blurs. However, when you use the glass to take a close look at something, the image is magnified.

When making or fitting small parts, tracing problems in mechanisms, and maintaining the cutting edges of tools, it's very helpful to see more. The glass reveals features invisible to the unaided eye.

Habitat: Woodworker's toolbox and Sherlock Holmes costume kit. Sold by hardware stores and home centers.

Primary Uses: Taking a close look at a small object. In medical emergencies, locating splinters embedded in the skin.

Secondary Uses: Igniting fires by concentrating sunlight on a spot—in social emergencies, you can start an afternoon barbecue or bonfire with a magnifying glass, but don't wait until too late in the day.

Variations: Jewelers and wood-carvers prefer a head-mounted binocular magnifier. Photographers, printers, and weavers use a small magnifying lens mounted in a bracket that maintains optimum viewing distance from their work.

How to Use: 1. **Magnification comes at the expense of brightness, so set up a strong work light.**

2. **Grasp the magnifying glass by its handle. Hold the workpiece in your other hand.**

3. **Look at the workpiece through the magnifying glass. Vary the distance until the view sharpens and clarifies. Arrange the light for a shadow-free look at the features of interest.**

99a–b. 📷 **MALLET**

General Description: *A cylindrical lump of wood, or head, with a handle sticking out of it.* On mallets preferred by cabinetmakers, the handle and head make a T. On mallets preferred by wood-carvers, the handle enters one end of the cylindrical head.

Habitat: Toolbox of cabinetmaker or woodcarver. Sold by home centers, hardware stores, and specialty tool dealers. Distinguish mallets from sledgehammers by their lighter weight and wood or plastic construction.

Primary Use: Imparting motion to tools or parts without also imparting damage.

Secondary Uses: Hammering dents out of sheet metal. Cracking walnuts. Tenderizing beefsteaks.

Variations: Dead-blow mallets, which are made of plastic with a shot-filled head, don't rebound. Mechanics' mallets have plastic faces so they don't damage soft metals or delicate gizmos.

How to Use: 1. Choose a situation where a blow from the mallet
might improve things—for example, two wooden
parts that ought to go together but don't quite, or the
interlocking pieces of a child's toy that arrived with
"some assembly required."

2. Place one of the parts flat on the worktable. Set the
other part in position.

3. Tap one part with the mallet, using just the mallet's
own weight. Inspect the situation to see whether the
desired motion has begun.

4. If appropriate motion has occurred, repeat the mallet
action (you might have to intensify the blows) until
you get the results you want.

5. If appropriate motion has not occurred, adjust the
angle between the parts, and/or the size of the larger
one, and repeat Steps 2 through 4. Usually it is best
to make one adjustment at a time.

100.   **MARKING GAUGE**

General
Description: *A square stick of wood about as long as an adult hand
that passes through a hole in a second piece of wood.* A
sharp metal point, called the "beam," sticks out near
one end of the square stick. The second piece of

wood, which is called the "head," has a thumbscrew in it. When you loosen the thumbscrew, you can slide the head along the beam. Tightening the thumbscrew locks the pieces.

Habitat: Woodworker's bench or toolbox. Sold by hardware stores and specialty tool outlets. Identification is easy because the general form of the marking gauge is unique, though there are several types of gauge.

Primary Use: Scratching a line on the workpiece parallel to an edge. Once the gauge has been set, it can mark many pieces to the same dimension.

Variations: A cutting gauge has a small knife in place of the sharp point and is used for cutting lines across the grain of the wood as well as for splitting thin wood with the grain. (For a discussion of wood grain see handsaw, page 202). A mortise gauge has a pair of points on one side of the stock, plus a single point on the opposite face, and it is used for marking the various dimensions of mortise and tenon joints without resetting.

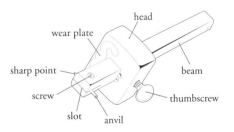

How to Use: 1. **Loosen the thumbscrew and slide the head of the gauge to the distance you wish to mark. Tighten the thumbscrew.**

2. **Hold the gauge by its head so the beam is horizontal. Rest your thumb on one edge of the head, with all four fingers on the opposite edge. Orient the gauge so its point is nearest your index finger and thumb and pointing down toward the wood. Hold the workpiece in your other hand.**

3. **Reach to start the gauge at the far end of the workpiece. Press its face against the edge, then roll the head so the gauge point makes contact.**

4. **Keeping the head pressed against the workpiece, draw the gauge toward your body.**

5. **Examine the workpiece to ensure the line you wanted has been scribed. If not, repeat Steps 3 and 4 but roll the head so the point digs in a little deeper.**

101.   **PLANE**

General Description: *An iron casting with one flat side, one or two wooden handles, and a complex mechanism trapping a sharp blade.* A plane is about the size and shape of an adult shoe. A narrow slot is set in the flat sole of the plane, and the edge of the blade sticking through it is just barely visible. A knurled brass knob about the size of a half-dollar is mounted close to the iron casting; a metal lever sticks up above everything else. When you turn the brass knob, the sharp blade moves minutely up and down in the narrow slot. When you move the lever from side to side, the sharp blade tilts minutely along with it. The tool's toggle can be loosened though it may seem quite stiff; when you do so, the blade loosens and comes out. With the blade removed you'll see that it was firmly bedded in the iron casting against a metal slope called the "frog."

A plane is a sophisticated contraption for holding a chisel at just the right angle for paring wood. Planes date at least to Roman times. The skills of planecraft are fundamental to making solid-wood furniture, though in this age of plywood and sanders, you can install doors and windows, trim rooms, and make built-ins and cabinets without ever touching one. Like handsaws, Western planes are designed to be pushed across the wood. Japanese planes—which have wooden bodies and no handles—are designed to be pulled. This contrast between West and East mirrors the difference between wrestling and martial arts.

Habitat: Woodworker's bench and toolbox. Sold by tool specialists. Though planes come in many sizes and shapes, they all have a blade held tightly in a block with its sharp edge emerging through a narrow slot.

Primary Use:	Flattening a wooden surface by peeling one thin shaving at a time (called "planing"), leaving a smooth surface behind. Paring the sharp corners off a piece of wood (called "chamfering").
Secondary Uses:	Paring the ends of a door that scrapes its jamb. Making the edge of a piece of wood square with respect to its face, one shaving at a time.
Operating Principle:	The plane is a self-jigging tool—it pares the wood to match the shape of its own flat sole. A plane cannot function without a razor-sharp edge on its blade. A sharp plane can make a shaving .002 inches (.005 cm) thick.
Variations:	Block planes are not as long as an adult hand; jack and smooth planes are the midsized general-purpose tools discussed here; the largest planes, almost as long as the adult arm, are called "jointers" (because they're used to flatten the long edges of wood for gluing together). Old planes have wooden bodies without blade-adjusting mechanisms. Planes with outriggers are for making moldings and grooves. Planes for making barrels and violins have curved soles. A spokeshave has a very small sole and blade and features handlebars. The sole of a compass plane is flexible and can be adjusted to fit the inside and outside edges of circles. Old planes are highly collectible, usually by old geezers.

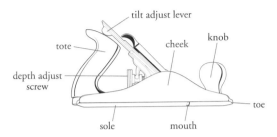

How to Use: 1. To make a piece of wood flat and smooth, choose a jack or smooth plane about as long as an adult hand. Be sure it is sharp.

2. Adjust the plane so the blade just barely protrudes through its slot and does not tilt.

3. Set the workpiece flat on the workbench, its far end butted against a stop.

4. Take a marching stance alongside the workbench. Plant the front of the plane sole (its toe) on the near end of the workpiece.

5. Push the plane along the wood.

6. If the plane makes a nice shaving, it's working, so continue until you're satisfied with the surface. If the shaving is uneven or ragged, check and adjust the blade and its tilt. If the wood tears up, you're planing

against the grain (see handsaw, page 202, for a discussion of grain). Turn the wood end for end and try
again.

7.   **If, despite fiddling, the plane will not make a shaving, sharpen the blade and repeat Steps 2 through 6.**

Tool-Kit   With one small, sharp plane you can trim sticking
Minimum: doors and drawers and remove any sharp corners.

102a–d. 📷   **RASP**

General   *A long, skinny piece of steel studded with sharp little*
Description: *burrs, or teeth.* A rasp has a wooden handle on one
               end. If you haven't used a rasp, you'll be surprised by
               how quickly it can shape a piece of wood, provided
               it's used with vigor and not tentatively.

Habitat: Woodworker's bench or toolbox and wood-carver's
               kit. Sold by hardware stores and home centers. Rasps
               have much larger, and thus fewer, teeth than files.
               Like files, they have one flat end and one that termi-
               nates in a long point called a "tang," which fits into a
               wood or plastic handle.

Primary   Freehand shaping and leveling of wood, fiberboard, or
Use: plastic by systematic abrasion. Rasps are for the mid-
               dle step between the rough-sawn surface left by a

chain saw or jigsaw and the smooth surface created by planing or sanding.

Variations: A shoemaker's rasp has four different tooth patterns on it. Sculptors' rifflers are small rasps curved and bent into various useful shapes. Instead of teeth, a Surform rasp is studded with many sharp-edged little holes, like a cheese grater.

Safety Note: A rasp without a handle poses extreme danger to the operator's hand because if it were to catch on a knot in the wood, the pointed tang might be driven into the operator's flesh, requiring not only stitches but also a tetanus shot.

How to Use: 1. **Choose a rasp that has a handle on its tang, or install one.**

2. **Draw the shape you want to create on the workpiece. Secure the workpiece with clamps (page 2) or in a vise (page 235).**

3. **Grip the handle in your dominant hand. Hold the far end of the rasp between your other thumb and index finger.**

4. **Push the rasp across the workpiece, then lift it for the return stroke. Push hard so it takes a good bite.**

5. **Continue to rasp the workpiece until you have ground it down to your layout line.**

103. 📷 **ROUTER**

General
Description:

A heavy metal can about the size of your head mounted on a flat, circular base plate with two handles. A hole is situated in the middle of the base plate, and inside you'll see a fat hexagonal nut screwed onto a shaft emerging from the bottom of the metal can. Features include an on/off switch, a locking mechanism for adjusting the height of the can on its base, and an electrical cord. When you plug the cord in and turn the switch on, the machine makes a noise that quickly revs up to a high pitch, and the hexagonal nut—the router's chuck—rotates very fast.

The electric router, which did not exist before the middle of the twentieth century, has almost totally replaced special-purpose planes for cutting moldings and grooves. Though some traditionalists lament this change, most woodworkers love their router and the labor it can save.

Habitat: Woodworker's toolbox and bench, usually found along with router bits. Sold by hardware stores and home centers. Distinguish the router from other rotating power tools by its large, flat base with a centered chuck.

Primary Uses:	Rounding the edges of a piece of wood, fiberboard, or plastic. Cutting a shape along the edge of a piece of wood. Cutting a groove or slot in the surface of a piece of wood.
Secondary Uses:	When coupled with a template, reproducing the shape of the template in one or more pieces of wood. Routers can also cut fiberboard and solid countertop materials like Corian. Special spiral bits are needed for aluminum.
Operating Principle:	A small cutter rotating at a very high speed can remove wood one tiny shaving at a time, leaving a smooth surface behind. A router cannot be used free-hand; it must be guided. There are seven different ways to guide a router, but the most basic is the one detailed below under "How to Use."
Variations:	Routers come in a wide variety of sizes, from small laminate trimmers that can be used one-handed up to 5-horsepower behemoths designed to be mounted under a worktable with the bit sticking up. Router chucks come in two standard sizes. Though the standard router base is a round piece of black plastic, some routers have square bases.
	A small handplane, the router is used for flattening the bottom of grooves and housings. In computer networks and the Internet, a router is the electronic hub through which devices interconnect.

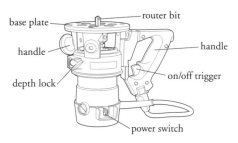

base plate — router bit

handle — handle

depth lock — on/off trigger

power switch

How to Use: 1.   **Choose a router bit (page 223) whose shape matches what you desire in the workpiece.**

2.   **Disconnect the router from its electrical supply and insert the bit in its chuck. Tighten the chuck according to the owner's manual—some routers use two wrenches, some have a locking lever with a single wrench, and some can be hand tightened.**

3.   **Adjust the height of the router so the portion of the bit you wish to use extends beyond the base plate.**

4.   **Measure the distance from the edge of the router bit to the edge of the router's base plate, and clamp a guide fence that distance away from the edge of the workpiece.**

5.   **Rest the base of the router on the workpiece but make sure the bit doesn't touch. Don your safety glasses and switch the router on.**

6. Slide the router across the workpiece until the edge of its base touches the guide fence.

7. Advance the router along the guide fence so the router bit cuts into the workpiece. When you move the router in one direction there is resistance, while in the other direction the cutting action tends to pull the router forward. Choose the direction in which you feel resistance—it's both safer and more accurate.

8. Shut the router off and wait for it to stop turning before you lift it to inspect the cut.

Tool-Kit Minimum: You need a router once you decide to try making your own furniture and woodworking projects.

104a–d. 📷

ROUTER BITS

General Description: *Small steel fingers with one cutting edge.* One end of a router bit is a perfectly round shaft. The other end has one or two cutting edges, and in a batch of bits some edges will be straight, some will be simply curved, and some will be intricately shaped. Some have ball bearings mounted on their shafts.

No matter what their shape, the router bits go with the electric router, and they are for cutting their own shape (or its inverse) into the edge of a piece of wood.

Habitat: | Woodworker's toolbox and bench, usually found adjacent to an electric router. Sold by hardware stores and home centers. Distinguish router bits from drill bits by their straight cutting edges (vs. helical). They're also relatively shorter and fatter.

Primary Use: | The router bit determines what shape the router will make in the workpiece.

Operating Principle: | The King Gillette principle: Give the razors away, and make your fortune selling replacement blades. Old and cheap router bits were made of high-speed steel, but almost all recently manufactured router bits have edges made of tungsten carbide, an extremely hard material that holds its sharpness. Though router bits with carbide inserts last a long time, they can't easily be sharpened and must be replaced when worn down.

How to Use: 1. **Choose a router bit whose shape matches the shape you want to cut, with a ball bearing pilot mounted below the cutting edge. Rounding the edges of a piece of wood or milling an ogee shape into an edge are examples of shaping tasks.**

2. **Seat the bit in the router and tighten it according to the owner's manual.**

3. **Adjust the router's depth of cut so the portion of the bit's edge that you wish to replicate emerges below**

the base plate. Check to see that the ball bearing pilot on the bit will ride against the edge of the workpiece without getting hung up on anything.

4. Put on your safety glasses, switch the router on, and cut the workpiece to shape by guiding the bit's ball bearing against the edge of the workpiece. For a discussion of which direction to drive, see Step 7 under router (page 220).

Tool-Kit Minimum: Once you own a router, buying bits is like buying CDs and DVDs: You can't ever have enough.

---

105. **SANDING BLOCK**

General Description: *A hard rubber block smaller than an adult hand, flat on one side and curved on the other, with slots at both ends.* Folding the rubber back from either slot reveals the points of three short nails embedded in the block.

Sanding blocks are sized to accept one-quarter of a standard letter-sized sheet of sandpaper. A strip of sandpaper anchors on the nails in the slots. The block's rubber sole, flat but minutely resilient, helps you finish-sand flat and curved surfaces, and cope with small irregularities in the surface.

A careful operator with a hand sanding block and an assortment of sandpapers almost always achieves a smoother and more thoroughly sanded surface than a casual operator using an electrically powered sander. Hand-sanding is an essential preparatory step when varnishing fine furniture and moldings.

Habitat:

Toolbox of woodworker, drywall technician, and painter. Sold by hardware stores, home centers, and paint stores. Usually found in the vicinity of letter-sized sandpaper sheets.

Primary Use:

Smoothing wooden surfaces and shapes after rough-ing with coarser tools and before final finishing.

Secondary Uses:

Preparing intermediate coats of varnish or paint for the final coat. Smoothing drywall between filler appli-cations and before painting.

Variations:

Before synthetic rubber, furniture finishers used flat chunks of cork as sanding blocks. Some sanding blocks have rolls of sandpaper mounted on an inter-nal mechanism, but they are not easy to change.

How to Use: 1.

Before varnishing a piece of furniture, clean the work space by sweeping or vacuuming dust and debris. Clear an area large enough for you to rotate the workpiece, bringing each surface uppermost.

2.

Begin with 100-grit sandpaper. Use a straight edge to tear the sheet into four equal strips. Tear across the short dimension of the sheet.

3. To load the sanding block, center its flat side on a strip of sandpaper, abrasive side down. Lift the rubber above one of the slots in the block and tuck the end of the sandpaper strip into it, pressing down on the rubber to seat the paper on the metal nails. Pull the paper tight around the block and repeat at the other end.

4. Rub the sanding block on each surface. Sand in the same direction as the grain, not across it. Pay extra attention to rough spots.

5. Brush the dust off the workpiece and vaccuum it up.

6. Repeat Steps 3 through 6 using 150-grit sandpaper, then repeat again using 220-grit. That's fine enough for most situations. For baby-bum smoothness on dense plastic and hard woods such as maple, continue through 320-grit and 400-grit paper.

Note: With all methods of sanding it is best to begin with coarse abrasive, work the entire surface, and to clean it off before switching to the next-finer abrasive. Proceed through all the available grits until you achieve the smoothness you want. When sanding old paint and between coats of varnish, the sandpaper is liable to clog. Use a wire brush to remove clogs lest they plough deep scratches in the workpiece.

106a–d.

SHARPENING STONE

General
Description:

A smooth brick that looks and feels like unpolished stone.
Sharpening stones, also known as oilstones or whet-
stones, are brown and about as long as your closed
hand, though only half as wide.

Man-made sharpening stones consist of uniformly
fine grains of a hard, abrasive material such as aluminum oxide embedded in a block of softer stuff;
natural stones, which are increasingly rare and expen-
sive, are quarried from the mineral novaculite.
Diamond sharpening stones, which have a coating of
industrial diamond dust bonded to a metal plate, produce results equivalent to regular sharpening stones,
and cut more quickly.

Aside from their composition, sharpening stones
are distinguished by whether they use a light mineral
oil or water as a lubricant. Japanese sharpening stones,
which are softer than Western ones, always use water
and commonly are stored submerged in a bucket.

Habitat:

Woodworker's toolbox or workbench. Sold by hardware stores, home centers, and tool specialists.
Grindstones and pumice stones for cleaning cooktops
are much coarser than sharpening stones.

Primary
Use:

Creating or restoring a sharp edge on steel blades and
tools. To determine if the edge is sharp, look straight
at it with strong light coming over your shoulder. A

dull edge bounces light back at you, but a sharp edge is invisible—it reflects no light.

Secondary Uses:
Flattening and polishing the soles, faces, and other working surfaces of such tools as planes and chisels.

Operating Principle:
A sharp edge occurs when two flat, smooth surfaces meet at a shallow angle like the point of a long, narrow wedge. Most woodworking tools have a sharp angle ranging between 25 and 35 degrees.

Variations:
Sharpening stones range from palm sized up to the length and width of the adult foot. Some stones are designated "coarse," "medium," or "fine." Others use number systems indicating fineness. These ratings range from 200 to 8,000, with higher numbers indicating finer abrasive particles; a Western 1,200-grit stone is approximately equivalent to a Japanese 4,000-grit stone.

How to Use: 1.
The key to sharpening a woodworking tool is to maintain both of the edge-forming surfaces originally ground into the tool, and to keep those surfaces truly smooth and flat. Use your magnifying glass to take a close look at the edge you intend to sharpen. In the case of planes and chisels, the flat side of the blade is one of the edge-forming surfaces, and a bevel ground at about 30 degrees is the other.

2.   Begin sharpening on a coarse (200-grit to 400-grit) stone. Place the stone flat on a worktable and soak its surface with the right lubricant, water or light oil.

3.   Hold the back of the tool flat on the sharpening stone, press down near the cutting edge, and move it back and forth from one end to the other. The objective is making the back flat and smooth.

4.   Turn the tool over to sharpen the bevel. Hold it at an angle so the factory bevel sits flat on the surface of the stone, then raise it a hair. Work the bevel back and forth from one end of the stone to the other, without changing its angle. Keep the stone lubricated.

5.   Assess your progress by looking at the metal. It will take on a dull sheen where the stone has cut into it. When the dull sheen reaches the very edge on both surfaces, it's time to move on to a finer stone.

Tool-Kit   Whether woodworking, cooking, or thinking, a sharp
Minimum: edge makes the difference.

---

107.   **TABLE SAW**

General   *A waist-high metal stand with a flat iron tabletop*
Description: *mounted on it and a dinner plate–sized saw blade stick-ing up through an opening.* The table saw has two shal-

low slots milled in the tabletop surface, plus a guard apparatus over the blade opening. A substantial beam crosses from one side of the table to the other. Under the table are large red and green on/off buttons, two handwheels mounted on adjacent sides of the stand, and an electrical cord.

This is the standard woodworking machine for cutting solid wood and sheets of plywood. Inside the opening in the tabletop you'll see either the circular saw blade or the horizontal shaft (called the "arbor") on which a blade would be mounted. The side-to-side beam is the saw's rip fence, which can be moved to different locations and locked in position. There might be a semicircular miter gauge in one of the table slots.

One handwheel raises and lowers the saw blade, while the other changes its tilt. Pushing the green "on" button starts the saw's electric motor and makes the circular blade rotate at a high speed. When idle, the machine emits a low hum; when cutting, the sound rises to a loud screech.

Habitat: Workshop of woodworker or cabinetmaker or on a builder's job site. Sold by home centers and specialty dealers. Though superficially similar to other machines for working with wood and metal, the table saw may be positively identified by its circular, dinner plate-sized saw blade and horizontal blade-mounting shaft.

Primary Use:	Cutting wood on a straight line, either across the grain (crosscutting to length) or with the grain (ripping to width).
Secondary Uses:	Cutting wood at various angles, usually for making rafters, stairs, or moldings. In many shops, the table saw serves as a convenient auxiliary work surface.
Operating Principle:	The table configuration with the blade mounted underneath is more versatile than the chop saw, more accurate than the jigsaw, and safer than the portable circular saw.
Variations:	Builders favor a lightweight table saw, called a "contractor's saw," that can be moved from job site to job site; these saws have a semi-enclosed base with the motor mounted off the back side. Cabinetmakers favor a heavy saw with a fully enclosed base that remains in one place in the workshop, usually surrounded by auxiliary worktables the same height.
Safety Note:	A high-speed circular saw can cut flesh as easily as it cuts wood. It is also capable of throwing a piece of wood back at the operator with deadly force.

It is essential that the saw has a blade guard mounted on it, either factory installed or an aftermarket add-on. The blade guard helps the operator keep his or her hands out of harm's way.

Saws sold in North America have a splitter (also |

called a "riving knife") mounted in-line with the blade as part of the guard assembly. Saws sold in Europe have a separate riving knife mounted directly on the blade mechanism. The splitter helps prevent kickback, an unpredictable accident that occurs when the back side of the saw blade catches the wood and hurls it toward the operator. The European splitter mounting system is safer and more versatile, while the American system is cheaper to manufacture.

It is very dangerous to operate a table saw without a guard and splitter. Though it is common to find table saws without guards and splitters in place, do not operate one that way. Also, be sure to wear eye and ear protection whenever you use a table saw.

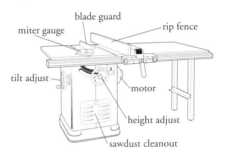

How to Use: 1. **Before you use the table saw, unplug it and follow the manufacturer's directions for installing a suitable blade. Reinstall the blade guard and splitter before you reconnect the electrical supply.**

2. To rip a piece of wood to width, move the saw's rip fence that distance from the blade and lock it. Raise the blade so the gullets between the saw teeth rise above the top of the workpiece.

3. Put on your eye and ear protection. With the saw turned off, rehearse the saw cut by pressing the workpiece against the saw fence and pushing it toward the saw blade. If kickback were to occur, the wood or the offcut would fly straight back from the saw blade. Eyeball that path and take a stable stance to the right or the left, out of harm's way.

4. Determine how close to the blade your fingers will be, and decide whether you will need to use a push stick for safety. A push stick is a length of wood or plastic with a notch in one end. It allows the operator to control and advance the wood from a safe distance.

5. Turn the saw on. Press the wood against the saw fence and advance it into the blade, using a push stick if necessary.

6. At the end of the cut, do not reach over the spinning blade to catch the wood. Instead, let it slide onto an auxiliary table you cleverly placed behind the saw, or let it fall onto the floor. Switch the saw off, then walk around to retrieve the workpiece and the offcut.

Tool-Kit
Minimum:
Serious woodworkers and professional builders consider a table saw essential.

108. 📷   **VISE**

General
Description:
A heavy apparatus consisting of two foot-sized cast-iron plates mounted on three substantial steel rods. Two of the bench vise's rods are smooth while the middle rod has coarse, square threads cut into it. One of the cast-iron plates has a stout T-shaped handle emerging from it. The other has two U-shaped slots cut in it.

When detached from a workbench, a bench vise is about knee-high if stood on end. Mounted in its normal position beneath the front edge of a workbench, the handle and the two iron plates (plus protective wooden facings fastened to the plates) are all that's visible—the remainder of the vise extends out of sight beneath the bench. When you turn the handle, the iron plates (called "jaws") move closer together or farther apart. Most vises have a split nut on the threaded rod, which facilitates opening the vise rapidly without a lot of handle turning.

Habitat:
Woodworker's bench. Sold by hardware stores, home centers, and tool specialists. The T-shaped handle and substantial iron jaws confirm identification as a vise; clamps (page 2), which have a similar action, are smaller and have a single bar instead of three rods.

Unlike a clamp, the vise is useless unless it's securely mounted beneath a workbench.

Primary
Use:

Firmly holding a workpiece in one position so it can be worked on with other tools.

Secondary
Uses:

Holding two or more workpieces together while glue dries. Pressing flowers. Cracking coconuts.

Operating
Principle:

Like a clamp, the bench vise gets its squeeze from turning a rod that has threads cut in it. The amount of squeeze a vise can exert depends on the relative diameter of the threaded rod, the length of handle, and the spacing of the threads.

Variations:

A metalworker's vise mounts on the bench rather than under it. It has smaller jaws and a built-in anvil. Old cabinetmaker's benches may have an all-wood vise instead of a metal one.

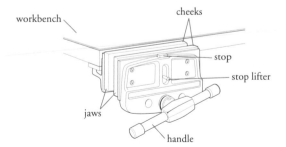

workbench

cheeks

stop

stop lifter

jaws

handle

How to Use: 1.   **Open the jaws of the vise wider than the workpiece.**

2.   **Place the workpiece between the jaws and turn the T handle to bring the jaws up to the workpiece.**

3.   **Adjust the workpiece into position.**

4.   **Tighten the handle so the vise jaws grip and squeeze the workpiece. Test it by wiggling. If it moves, tighten the jaws some more.**

Tool-Kit Minimum: If you have a workbench, it needs a vise.

109.   **WORKBENCH**

General Description: *A substantial four-legged table, with a vise mounted beneath the top.* The top of a workbench has to be rigid and stiff, and at least as thick as three fingers held close together. While you can buy a sturdy bench, most woodworkers ultimately make their own, building in personal details to suit their own style of working.

Habitat: Woodworker's shop. Sold by tool specialists. Distinguish from worktables by the thicker top and the presence of a vise.

Primary Use:	Holding the workpiece so you can work on it.
Operating Principle:	The bench is your island of stability in a sea of uncertainty. You can't do accurate work on something that moves. The thicker and heavier the bench, the better.
Variations:	Handy homeowners often prefer a storage bench, which is lighter with many drawers underneath and along the back of the top. A worktable is also lighter than a bench, and often has a larger top; worktables made specifically for assembling furniture may be quite low to the ground. A portable work stand may have a built-in vise, but it is smaller and lighter than a workbench so it can be moved around a job site. A cabinetmaker's bench may have a trough or well along the back edge to catch small tools and hardware.

stop   fixed top
vise   movable top
handle
tilt latch
fold latch
leg

How to Use: 1. **Always use the vise, clamps, or stops to anchor the workpiece on the bench.**

2. **For heavy pounding, place the workpiece over one of the bench legs.**

3. **For pushing sideways, for example, when using a hand plane, butt the workpiece against a stop that's clamped, nailed, or screwed to the top of the bench.**

4. **For sawing or carving, trap the workpiece in the bench vise.**

5. **When working on oily mechanisms, as well as when painting and varnishing, protect the surface of the bench with a cover made from a tough, thin material such as fiberboard or plywood.**

VIII. Fasteners

Fasteners are the stuff that hold our lives together. Nails, screws, glue, ties, hinges, and nuts and bolts can create temporary or permanent connections between all your parts.

110.

CABLE TIES

General Description:

Flat and skinny strips of tough plastic with a square socket formed on one end. Both sides of the indestructible plastic strips have tiny laddered grooves molded into the surface except for a finger's width at the small end, which is smooth and has a rounded tip.

The square socket has an opening the same size as the plastic strip, with a plastic tooth inside. When you poke the small end of the strip into the square socket, it feeds easily and makes clicking sounds. When you try to withdraw it, you can't—nothing happens, it's stuck tight. Although meant for bundling electronic wires together, cable ties have other uses as well.

Habitat:

Toolbox of electrician, handyperson, or electronic hobbyist. Sold by hardware stores and home centers. Distinguish cable ties from bag ties by their toughness, laddered surface, and square socket.

Primary Use:	Controlling and tidying the many wires involved with computers, audiovisual equipment, and cars. The cable-tied assembly of all the wires in a car is called a "wiring harness."
Secondary Uses:	Making holiday wreaths or hanging garlands. Tightly bundling chopsticks, barbecue skewers, or knitting needles. In civil emergencies, police use a form of cable tie as handcuffs.
Operating Principle:	The precise geometry of the square socket and laddered strip guarantees one-way action: Take a close look with your magnifying glass. You can't undo a cable tie; you have to cut it.
Variations:	Cable ties come in many colors and sizes.

How to Use: 1. **Gather all of the loose wires you would like to contain in a bundle.**

2. **Wrap the bundle with a single cable tie set near to the largest equipment connected to a wire (computer or television, for example). Don't tighten the tie yet. Use the smallest tie that wraps around the bundle.**

3. **Add more ties a hand span apart along the bundle. Make them snug but do not tighten; it should be easy to adjust the wires. Allow each wire to leave the bundle as needed to reach its destination.**

4. **If there is excess cable, double it back on itself and fasten it with additional cable ties.**

5. **When all the cables have reached their destinations, go back along the bundle to smooth out kinks, optimize the route, and tighten all the ties. To anchor the bundle at any point, loop a tie around a screw driven into a supporting surface.**

6. **Use wire cutters (page 128) to remove any errant cable ties, and also to clip each free end off close to its socket.**

Tool-Kit
Minimum:

Like other tools that initially seem unnecessary, in the twenty-first–century electronic household, cable ties are hard to live without.

111a–e.

GLUE

General
Description:

A viscous, sticky liquid that creates a permanent bond when dry. Glue is housed in small containers; the caps of these containers are removable. Nothing immediately happens upon removal of the cap, but if you upend the container and shake or squeeze it, the glue dribbles out. There's no way to get the glue back into the container. If you leave it alone for a while, the spilled glue begins to thicken and then to harden.

When spread on two objects that are then pressed

together for a time, the glue hardens and the two pieces bond. Some glues harden in a few seconds while others take overnight to set and weeks to fully cure. The liquid phase of glue is temporary; the hard phase is permanent.

Habitat: All toolboxes and work areas as well as children's craft tables. Sold by hardware stores and home centers.

Primary Uses: Joining wood to wood, plastic to plastic, or fabric to fabric. Repairing broken objects. Dissimilar materials can be glued together, but the results are less certain than when gluing similar materials.

Secondary Uses: In social emergencies, glue can tack a cuff or hem in place, temporarily mend a broken denture or serving dish, install a wig, or persuade recalcitrant items of decor to stay in place. In medical emergencies, cyanoacrylate glue can repair a torn fingernail or close a cut while it heals—surgeons routinely use it. Pranksters also find quick-setting glue hard to resist.

Operating Principle: Glue doesn't just harden, it makes a molecular bond with the surfaces being joined. As they set, most glues change their composition, some by solvent evaporation, some by polymeric linking, some by a chemical reaction. In successful gluing operations the bond will be as strong or stronger than the joined materials.

Variations: There's a glue on the market for almost every conceivable material and purpose. Glue formerly was made by boiling animal hides and hoofs; brown hide glue is one of the few reversible glues and so is favored by antique restoration specialists. White craft glue and yellow woodworking glue are versatile polyvinyl acetate (PVA) formulas that will join wood, fabric, and leather, but not ceramic or plastic.

Cyanoacrylate glue (often sold as superglue) and urethane glue can join most materials including wood, glass, ceramics, metal, and some plastics, provided the parts make a near-perfect fit without glue. Two-part epoxy glue fills the gaps between parts that don't quite fit, and will stick to almost anything, including concrete. Epoxy is the best choice for dissimilar materials; slow-setting epoxies usually develop more ultimate strength than quick-set mixtures.

Vinyl and most other plastics require a specifically formulated glue. Use contact cement to stick plastic laminate on countertops; spray glue is contact cement for artwork.

Construction adhesive, which comes in a cylinder that fits your caulk gun, is for mounting insulation board, wall paneling, and mirror tiles.

How to Use: 1. **Choose a glue that's suitable for the materials you wish to join. For joining wood, choose yellow PVA glue.**

2. Make sure the surfaces you wish to join are smooth, clean, and fit tightly together without glue. Roughing up the surface before gluing results in a weaker bond than one made between smooth surfaces.

3. Joints made with yellow PVA glue should be tightly clamped together and left undisturbed to set. Yellow glue begins to cure in minutes, so there is no time for coffee in between spreading the glue and closing the assembly. Find suitable clamps and rehearse the operation before spreading the glue.

4. Spread a thin, uniform coating of glue on both surfaces. For small surfaces, spread with a flat stick or a small, disposable brush. On large surfaces, use a disposable paint roller.

5. Close and clamp the assembly. Small beads of glue should squeeze out of the joint. Major drools indicate excess generosity in Step 4.

6. After several hours, but before the glue completely sets, scrape off the squeezed-out glue.

7. Leave the assembly in clamps overnight.

Tool-Kit Minimum: Once opened, most types of glue begin to harden in the container, so purchase small amounts as needed. Keep a double tube of quick-setting two-part epoxy at the ready—it can be stored indefinitely after opening so long as the two components aren't allowed to mix.

112a–f.

HINGES

General
Description:

Flat pieces of metal with a cylinder attached across their middles. Holes in hinges go straight through from one side but are beveled wider on the other side. When you pick one up and try to flex it, the metal folds along the cylinder (called a "barrel"). The barrel is hollow, divided into tight-fitting sections, and another piece of metal (called a "pin") is inside it. On some hinges the pin can be removed—it looks like a fat nail—while on others it's fixed in place. When both flat pieces are attached to two different objects, those objects can be "hinged" toward or away from one another.

Habitat:

Toolbox of woodworker and builder. Sold by hardware stores and home centers. The ability to open and fold distinguishes hinges from other metal parts. They're sold in pairs, and usually installed in pairs.

Primary
Uses:

Mounting doors on houses and cabinets so that they may be opened and closed at will. Loose-pin hinges can be used to make knockdown furniture and assemblies of parts.

Operating
Principle:
The hinge pin is a pivot and its precise location controls how the door opens and swings, as well as
whether or not the door hangs up on adjacent parts.

Variations:
Hinges come in innumerable types, sizes, colors, and
finishes. Some are meant to be concealed while others
add interesting visual detail. A piano hinge is very
long, so you can cut it to the length of the parts being
connected. Cup hinges, common on built-in cabi-
netry, have a number of built-in adjustments govern-
ing their placement and how they open.

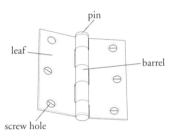

How to Use: 1.
**Choose hinges that are the right size and configura-
tion for your project. To hang a door on your broom
closet, you could use a pair of regular door hinges
(called "butts"), but a single piano hinge will be
much easier to install.**

2.
**Experiment with the door and hinge to see how it has
to be installed. With the door closed, the two leaves
of the hinge should also be closed together and con-**

cealed between the door and its frame with just the barrel sticking out. Make sure the hinge operation will match the direction the door should swing.

3. Measure the edge of the door and mark the length on your hinge.

4. Use a hacksaw (page 286) to cut the hinge to length.

5. Set the hinge along the edge of the door with its barrel overhanging the wood. Use two small clamps (page 2) to hold it in place.

6. Fasten the hinge onto the door with three screws at top, bottom, and center.

7. Position the door in the jamb and mark the location of the hinges. Fasten the other leaf of the hinge onto the door jamb with two screws at top and bottom.

8. Test the swing of the door. Make sure it opens and closes the way you want, without binding or sticking anywhere. If it's okay, drive the remaining screws into both leaves of the hinge. If not, remove the offending screws, reposition the parts (you may need to trim the edge of the door or add a shim or spacer under one of the hinge leaves), and try again.

113a–h. **NAILS**

General
Description:
Round sticks of metal considerably smaller in diameter than length. One end of a nail tapers to a small four-sided point that resembles a pyramid. At the other end of this formed metal shank is a flat disk (the head) that is wider than the shank. There are several tiny ridges in the shank just below the head.

Habitat:
Toolbox of builder, woodworker, or handyperson. Sold by hardware stores and home centers. Distinguish nails from screws and bolts by the absence of threads on the shank; distinguish them from hinge pins by the presence of a point on one end. Nails rarely are found in isolation; usually you'll find a box, jar, or cat food can full.

Primary
Use:
Joining two pieces of wood together by being hammered through one and into the other.

Secondary
Uses:
Decorating wood and leather surfaces; some African fetish objects are studded with hundreds of nails. In fashion emergencies, small nails can hold clothing in place as pins would.

Operating
Principle:
The point of the nail pushes the wood fibers aside and breaks some of them; it does not make a true hole. The nail stays in place because of friction between the wood fibers and the nail shank.

Variations: Nails are manufactured in an infinite variety of sizes, head shapes, and surface finishes. Galvanized nails have been dipped in zinc to resist rusting; marine nails for underwater use are made of stainless steel or bronze. Nails with a small head are for finish applications: the head can be driven below the surface of the wood with a nail set and the hole filled in with putty. Screw shank nails (the twist is much more gradual than screw threads) are for anchoring wooden flooring. Roofing nails have large, flat heads, while upholstery nails have decorative heads. Cut nails have a square shank and a blunt point. Before industrialization they were individually made by blacksmiths; if a building burned down, it was important to sift the ashes for nails that could be reused.

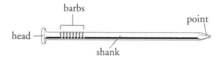

How to Use: 1.   **Choose nails that are long enough to go through one piece of wood and almost through the second piece, or if the second piece is thicker, at least to the thickness of the first piece.**

2.   **Use a pencil to make a layout line and mark the location of each future nail.**

3. Hold or clamp the two parts together and use a hammer (page 149) to drive the first nail into the workpiece. Hold it with one hand while you tap gently to start it, then get your fingers out of the way and deliver a few substantial swats. Try to drive the nail flush with the wood without making any hammer dents in the wood.

4. If necessary, adjust the arrangement of the parts. Then drive two more nails. Three nails is the right number for most applications; more won't make a stronger connection and might split the wood.

5. When you are using finishing nails, drive their heads just under the surface of the wood using a center punch (page 278) or nail set.

Note: To make a supertough nailed connection, choose nails that are long enough to penetrate both pieces of wood. Then hammer the protruding points over and down flat on the back side. This is called "clenching." Shacks built with clenched nails have been picked up by tornados and set down intact.

Tool-Kit Minimum: Buy boxes of nails as you need them; you'll soon accumulate a handy collection of sizes and shapes.

114a–f. 📷   **NUTS AND BOLTS**

General
Description:
Two connected pieces of hardware formed of metal; the hexagonal nut twists onto the threaded shank of a bolt. Bolts are short shanks of metal with a straight, uniform thread cut into them, a bulky head formed on one end, and a plain, flat end on the other. Hexagonal lumps of metal with threaded holes that twist onto the threaded shank are called nuts. Married to the nut and bolt are washers, thin metal disks with centered holes that fit over the metal shaft and slide up to the head.

Habitat:
Toolbox and workbench of mechanic, woodworker, or builder. Sold by hardware stores, home centers, and auto parts stores. Distinguish bolts from nails by the presence of threads on the shank; from screws by the absence of a point. Nuts and washers fit on bolts and usually are found nearby.

Primary
Use:
Making firm but reversible connections between wood, metal, or plastic parts.

Operating
Principle:
The thread on a bolt is a long, slow wedge conferring large mechanical advantage. Bolts minutely stretch as they tighten.

Variations:
Like screws and nails, bolts are manufactured in infinite variety. Some are long, some are fat, some are

thin, and some are short. There are bolts with coarse threads, fine threads, square threads, or metric threads. While most have hexagonal heads, some have round, flat heads with hexagonal sockets. Bolts are identified by diameter, thread style, and head type.

Washers look like coins with a hole in the center. Locking washers are star-shaped or cut from edge to hole and sprung. Tightening a nut and bolt onto either kind of lock washer makes the points of the star, or of the cut, grip the surfaces.

Nuts are usually hexagonal but some are square; some have winglike extensions for finger tightening; and some incorporate a cap on the end of the thread. Nuts are not interchangeable, except that fortuitously a $^5/16$-inch coarse-threaded nut will fit an 8-mm metric bolt. Nuts are not affected by the length of the bolt, only by its diameter and thread style.

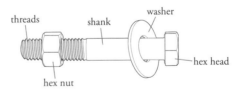

How to Use: 1. **Choose a bolt that is long enough to pass completely through both connecting parts, but not so long that the bare shank above the threads emerges.**

2. If the parts do not already have holes in them, drill suitable holes. Holes for bolts should be a hair larger than the outside diameter of the threads; check by drilling a test hole or by measuring with your dial caliper.

3. Bolts work best when there are two washers on the shank, one under the head and one against the nut. Fit the first washer onto the bolt, slide it up to the head, then fit the bolt into the hole through both workpieces.

4. Add the second washer and turn the nut onto the bolt. If you are going to use a lock washer, it goes under the nut. Make the assembly finger tight.

5. Install additional bolts, washers, and nuts as necessary.

6. Verify the alignment of the parts and adjust, if necessary. Use two wrenches, one on the bolt head and the other on the nut, to tighten each part. When the last one is snug, revisit them all and retighten as needed.

115a–h. 📷 **SCREWS**

General
Description: *A round stick of metal with twisting grooves in its shank, which also form a twisted vane of metal called the*

"thread." One end of the shank tapers to a sharp point. A head appears on the other end, with a slot or a shaped depression in it.

The screw, a common fastener for wood and sheet metal, is much more secure than nails. Screws are meant to be driven by being turned with the aid of a screwdriver. As the screw turns, the threaded shank pulls it into the workpiece. A screw works best when you drill a pilot hole in the material to make room for the shank.

Habitat: Toolbox of builder, woodworker, or handyperson. Sold by hardware stores and home centers. Distinguish screws from nails by the presence of threads on the shank; distinguish them from bolts by the presence of a point on one end. Screws rarely are found in isolation, as they tend to be gathered together with other screws in boxes, baby food jars, or other convenient containers.

Primary Use: Joining two pieces of wood or sheet metal. Wood pieces joined with screws plus glue are married for life; you will not get the two pieces apart.

Secondary Uses: Fastening large sheets of drywall to the structure of the building. At the bar, make a royal screw by gently mixing equal parts cognac and orange juice, then filling the glass with chilled champagne.

Operating
Principle:

The sharp thread cuts its way into the workpiece, making it almost impossible to withdraw by pulling; it must be turned out the same way it went in (but in the opposite direction).

Variations:

As with nails, screws are manufactured in infinite varieties. The screw head may be round on top and flat on the underside or flat on top and tapered on the underside. The driving socket in the head may be a slot, a cross-shaped depression (called a "Phillips" or "cross-head" screw), or a square depression (called a Robertson or square-drive screw). A six-pointed star-shaped depression in the head indicates a Torx screw, developed by the automobile industry for assembly by robots. Galvanized screws are coated with zinc to resist rusting; marine screws are made of stainless steel. All wood screws come to a sharp point. Screws for sheet metal have a flat point with a sharp notch.

Small bolts are sometimes called "machine screws," but they cannot be installed without going into a threaded hole or a nut. Most machine screws have hexagonal heads like other bolts, but some have screw-style heads.

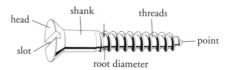

How to Use: 1. **To fasten one piece of wood to another, use three screws. Choose screws that are long enough to go through one piece and penetrate at least that far into the other piece, though not so far that they emerge on the back side. Choose a screwdriver (page 173) that fits the head of the screw.**

2. **Make layout lines and mark the location of each future screw on the top piece of wood.**

3. **Drill a pilot hole through the top piece at each layout mark. The pilot hole should be just large enough for the screw to fit through without having to be turned; you can measure the diameter of a screw as well as of a drill bit with your dial caliper (page 190).**

4. **Clamp the pieces of wood together. Insert the first screw and twist it home with the appropriate screwdriver. In hard woods, you might need to drill a second pilot hole in the second piece of wood. Make it slightly smaller than the root of the screw shank between the threads.**

5. **Check the alignment of the parts, adjust as necessary, and drive the remaining screws tight to the wood.**

Tool-Kit Minimum: When you find yourself using a lot of a particular size of screw, shop for a box containing 100 or more. Screws don't spoil and can be stored indefinitely.

IX. Plumbing

Residential plumbing involves three different kinds of pipes—iron, copper, and plastic—each with its own set of tools and working techniques. Plastic is by far the easiest for the handyperson, and would be the material of choice when renovating older houses. Connections between different kinds of pipe require special fittings and expert consultation.

Iron pipe makes threaded connections that become watertight by being twisted tightly together. It's cut with a hacksaw, threaded with taps and dies, and twisted together with pipe wrenches. The hard part is twisting the new connection without loosening previous ones, a push-pull ballet of two straining wrenches.

Copper pipe and copper connectors become watertight when glued together with a molten metal called solder; it's cut with a tubing cutter, then soldered using a propane torch. The metal has to be wire brushed clean and shiny, then heated, and the trick is getting it hot enough for the solder to flow into the joint without directing the flame on the clean metal.

Plastic pipe and plastic fittings become watertight when glued together with a gooey, quick-setting glue. It's easy to cut with a jigsaw, hacksaw, or fine-toothed handsaw, and to clean up with a file or a sharp knife. The glue goes on with a brush that comes attached to the lid on the can.

116a–b. **ADJUSTABLE PLIERS**

General
Description:

Two thick bars of steel crossed and joined with a stout bolt and nut. The bars, or handles, end in short jaws with serrated surfaces that are bent (cranked) 45 degrees out of line with the handles. The nut and bolt that form the pliers' pivot go through a long slot machined into one handle just below its jaw; the back side of this handle has a series of curved grooves machined into it as well. The grooves mate with a curved lug formed on the back side of the other handle, which the pivot bolt is attached to. When you open the handles as far as they'll go, it's possible to slip the lug from one groove to another, changing the opening between the jaws. At any opening, the serrated jaws remain more or less parallel.

Adjustable groove joint pliers (also called "water-pump pliers") are stable and not likely to slip their setting when in use (unlike two-position slip joint pliers, the ones with a figure eight at the knuckle). This feature, plus the cranked and parallel jaws, makes groove joint pliers suitable for plumbing. They're especially effective on shower heads and sink drains and traps.

Pliers and their close cousins—tongs, cutters, snips, and scissors—are ancient tools originally made to order by blacksmiths, who themselves could not have worked without tongs for manipulating the red-hot iron. Today pliers are industrially forged and

machined in a bewildering variety of sizes and specialized designs.

Habitat: Toolbox of plumber and mechanic. Sold by hardware
            stores, home centers, and auto parts stores. Groove
            joint pliers are manufactured in a wide range of sizes.

Primary   Tightening and loosening large fittings on plumbing
Use: and machinery.

How to Use: 1. **Choose groove joint pliers whose jaws will open far
                 enough to grip the fitting of interest.**

             2. **Open the jaws fully and slip the joint to the dimen-
                 sion of the part. To protect the finish, wrap chromed
                 plumbing in a rag.**

             3. **Set the pliers on the fitting so that pulling the han-
                 dles in the desired direction helps seat the fitting
                 deeper in the jaws. If they are oriented the wrong
                 way, pulling the handles will roll the fitting out of
                 the jaws.**

             4. **Push or pull the handles of the pliers to tighten or
                 loosen the fitting.**

             5. **Reposition the jaws. To open the jaws just enough for
                 repositioning, use your smallest finger slipped in
                 between the handles.**

| Tool-Kit Minimum: | One pair of 12-inch (30 cm) adjustable pliers will help you through most routine household plumbing. |

117.   **FAUCET PULLER**

| General Description: | *A Y-shaped, two-handled apparatus similar to a corkscrew with a straight, flat-ended rod instead of a screw.* The faucet puller is for gently lifting those expensive, nicely finished faucet handles off their internal workings so that leaks and drips can be repaired.
The rod connects to the upright base of the Y, which consists of a longer and thicker threaded rod with a T-shaped handle. A loose metal fitting connects a matched pair of L-shaped brackets (the arms of the Y) to the threaded rod. Turning the T-handle makes the fitting and the pair of brackets move up and down the threaded rod. |

| Habitat: | Plumber's truck or handyperson's toolbox. Sold by hardware stores and plumbing suppliers. |

| Primary Use: | Removing faucet handles without damaging them. |

| Operating Principle: | The faucet puller uses a threaded rod to transmit upward force to the underside of the faucet handle. |

Variations: Faucet pullers resemble the auto mechanic's gear and bearing puller and can be used on other small mechanisms too.

How to Use: 1. **Before resorting to a faucet puller, try to remove the handle by hand. Most faucets have a screw-on top, though it might be hidden under a cap that can be lifted by slipping a small screwdriver or a knife blade underneath. Close the sink drain so the screw won't be lost, then remove the screw with a suitable screwdriver. Grasp the handle and try to wiggle it straight up and off the valve.**

2. **Open the faucet puller until you can feed the flat-ended rod into the screw hole atop the faucet. Snuggle it under the faucet handle.**

3. **Turn the T handle until the faucet lifts off.**

118. **PIPE WRENCH**

General
Description:
A heavy bar of iron with a J-shaped jaw mounted on one end. The long part of the J passes loosely through a fitting mounted on the main handle, with a round, knurled nut inside. Turning the nut makes the J-shaped jaw move up and down. When you heft the wrench, its parts jangle and clack together.

Pipe wrenches (also called "Stilson wrenches") are

for working on iron pipe, that is, virtually all plumbing installed before 1950 in older houses and apartments. They have to be used in pairs: One wrench immobilizes the pipe while the other turns the fitting on or off. The loosely hinged movable jaw digs into the iron and self-tightens. Note that when oriented one way the teeth dig in, while when oriented the other way they slip the jaws off the pipe.

Habitat: Plumber's truck and handyperson's tool box. Sold by hardware stores, home centers, and plumbing suppliers; though pipe wrenches are used in pairs, they're not merchandised that way. The J-shaped jaw loosely attached to the handle is characteristic, as is the clack.

Primary   Installing and removing iron pipe and pipe fittings.
Use:

Variations: Pipe wrenches come in many sizes. Some old ones have wooden handgrips. New ones are painted with bright-colored enamel for easy spotting.

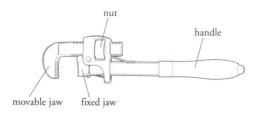

nut

handle

movable jaw   fixed jaw

How to Use: 1. **The male threads on the ends of iron pipe are tapered. They become watertight only when twisted as far as possible into the female threads inside elbows and couplings. When installing, paint the male threads on the pipe with pipe joint compound. Do not treat the female threads.**

2. **Choose a pipe wrench large enough for the pipe and a second wrench that matches the size of the fitting.**

3. **Hand twist the parts together as far as they will go. Then use one wrench to anchor the pipe while you twist the fitting with the other. As the joint tightens, you'll have to put as much clockwise force on one wrench as counterclockwise force on the other.**

4. **When uninstalling, reverse Step 3.**

Tool-Kit
Minimum: People who live in old houses need two or three pipe wrenches.

  119a–c. **PLUMBING WRENCHES**

General
Description: *Plumbing fixtures are so diverse and awkward to reach that installation and repair requires a variety of special-purpose wrenches.* A handyperson's box of plumbing tools is likely to include large groove joint pliers (page 259) plus three more essentials: a flange wrench (Y-

shaped, with one jaw that moves by way of a worm gear and a thumbscrew that locks it in position); a crowfoot wrench (a spring-loaded jaw on the end of a forearm-length rod with a T handle); and a nipple wrench (a short hexagonal bar of steel with a serrated eccentric cam on the end).

Habitat: Plumber's truck or handyperson's toolbox. Sold by hardware stores, home centers, and plumbing suppliers. Special-purpose plumbing wrenches are difficult to distinguish from specialty automotive wrenches—both can be used on either job.

Primary   The flange wrench (also called a "spud wrench")
Uses: adjusts to fit the broad, flat nut on the underside of the drain in sinks, tubs, and showers. You can't install or replace a drain without one.

   The crowfoot wrench (also called a "basin wrench" or "faucet wrench") helps you reach up behind a sink to get at the nearly inaccessible nuts underneath faucets, necessary to install or replace them. The nipple wrench grips the inside of short, threaded pipe connectors (nipples) so they can be installed or removed.

Variations: Strap wrenches and chain wrenches are large enough for black iron waste lines. When working on water supply tubes underneath a sink, look for the right-sized box wrenches because they won't slip, whereas adjustable crescent wrenches and adjustable pliers almost certainly will.

How to Use: 1. **Survey the available wrenches and make your best guess as to what might fit the plumbing.**

2. **Adjust the wrench to match the fitting; if the fitting is visible and has a polished surface, use tools with smooth jaws, or protect it with a rag.**

3. **Be sure you know which way the fitting needs to turn, clockwise usually tightens and counterclockwise loosens, but it's not always obvious or logical.**

4. **Seat the wrench firmly on the fitting and push or pull on the wrench to turn the fitting. It might take all your strength and more. It might turn only a tiny bit before the wrench has to be released and reseated.**

120. **PROPANE TORCH**

General Description: *A forearm-sized metal cylinder, painted bright blue, with a flat bottom and a bent brass pipe coming out the top.* A brass fitting with a black plastic knob connects the bent brass pipe to the blue cylinder. The bent pipe has a second fitting threaded onto its other end, which widens into a circular orifice, and there is a ring of holes in the metal just above the connection.

When you tap the cylinder it makes a hollow ringing sound. When you shake it, there seems to be fluid inside. When you turn the valve it makes a hissing sound and smells like rotten eggs.

Habitat: Plumber's truck or handyperson's toolbox. Sold by hardware stores, home centers, and plumbing suppliers. Small quantities of useful gases are sold in color-coded metal cylinders; bright blue is propane, green is oxygen, yellow is MAPP welding gas, and red is fire suppressant.

Primary Use: Making watertight joints in copper pipe by heating it until solder melts and flows.

Secondary Uses: Heating corroded iron fittings to loosen them. Breaking down hardened epoxy glue (via heat). Heating dried window putty or asphalt floor tile to soften and remove it. Killing weeds by scorching them. Caramelizing the sugar atop crème brûlée.

Operating Principle: Hydrocarbon gases such as propane burn hot when combined with oxygen from the air.

Variations: Some propane nozzles include a battery-powered electric lighter with an on/off switch. Propane valves and nozzles are not interchangeable with fittings meant for benzene and MAPP gas.

Safety Note: If you use too much solder, the excess will run out of the fitting and drip like water. While it is not likely to set off a fire, at 700+°F (300+°C), it is more than hot enough to cause a nasty burn, so be certain it does not drip on you. Plumbing pipe should only be soldered with plumbing solder, which does not contain lead. Don't use electrical solder on plumbing.

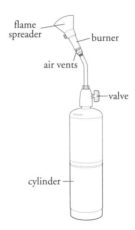

How to Use: 1.   **Screw a propane valve onto the threaded fitting atop the propane cylinder.**

        2.   **Clean the end of the copper pipe and the inside of the fitting with a wire brush and a strip of emery abrasive paper. Make the metal clean and shiny.**

3. **Paint the clean metal with soldering flux. Push the fitting together.**

4. **Put on your work gloves and safety glasses, then open the propane valve a little bit and ignite the flame using the built-in igniter or a spark lighter. Adjust the valve so the flame burns blue and yellow with a light blue cone in the middle. The tip of the inner cone is the hottest part of the flame.**

5. **Play the hot part of the flame on the outside of the copper fitting and on the pipe near the fitting. Touch the seam between them with the end of a piece of plumbing solder, keeping the solder out of the direct flame. When the metal is hot enough, the grey solder will abruptly flash bright silver and flow into the joint.**

6. **When the solder flows, take it away and shut off the torch. Wipe the joint with a rag to remove excess flux.**

Tool-Kit Minimum: One hot propane flame has a surprising number of uses.

121. 📷   **TUBING CUTTER**

General Description: *A silvery metal casting shaped like the letter E.* A threaded rod with a knob on its end passes through the base of a tubing cutter's E shape; the rod is connected to the middle part of the E, which also has two small rollers mounted on it. The top of the E has a small, free-turning disk mounted in it. The disk is sharpened all the way around its edge, like the cutter of a kitchen can opener. When you turn the knob on the threaded rod, the part with the rollers moves.

The tubing cutter makes a clean cut in copper pipe and other thin-walled metal tubing (it also works on some kinds of plastic pipe). There's a sharp V of flat metal protruding from the back side of the tool, which can be used as a reamer for removing swarf and burrs from the pipe.

Habitat:
Toolbox of plumber or handyperson. Sold by hardware stores, home centers, and plumbing suppliers. The geometry of the tubing cutter is not unique, so check for the sharp cutting wheel facing smooth rollers.

Primary Uses:
Cutting copper plumbing pipe. Cutting some kinds of plastic pipe and tubing.

Variations:
Each tubing cutter accepts a range of pipe sizes; one marked 3/16-inch (5 mm) to 1 1/8 inch (3 cm) OD (outside diameter) will handle most residential water supply lines. Some tubing cutters are hefty enough to cut iron pipe as well as copper.

How to Use: 1. **Choose a tubing cutter whose capacity matches the pipe.**

2. **Carefully measure the cutting line and mark it with a pencil, marker, or visible scratch.**

3. **Open the tubing cutter wide enough to accept the pipe. Move it so the wheel is directly on the cutting mark.**

4. **Tighten the knob to close the cutting wheel onto the pipe, then twist the cutter all the way around the pipe. Continue tightening and twisting until the cutter breaks through the inside of the pipe.**

5. **Clean the burr from the inside of the pipe using a reamer, file, or sharp knife.**

6. **Maintain the cutter with a little light oil on the threads and the axles of the cutter and rollers.**

Tool-Kit
Minimum: At least one is necessary in dwellings supplied by copper pipe.

X. Mechanical and Automotive

Mechanisms and assemblies such as cars, machines, and self-assembled consumer products are made of metal and hard plastic. Working on them involves cutting these unforgiving materials to size and shape, finishing their surfaces, connecting the parts, and installing suitable fasteners.

122. 📷 **BOLT CUTTER**

General Description:
Long, heavy handles that meet at a three-knuckle compound pivot. The handles of bolt cutters have rubber grips. The pivot connects the handles to a pair of sharp steel jaws that close precisely together. When you open the handles as far as they'll go, the jaws open wide enough to fit a pencil. When you close the handles, the jaws slowly close together until the stop on one handle bumps into the other.

Habitat:
Toolbox of builder or handyperson. Sold by hardware stores and home centers.

Primary Use:
Cutting through bolts and other iron bars.

Secondary Uses:
Cutting chain-link fence, thick power cables, and bicycle locks.

Operating Principle:	A bolt cutter uses an ingenious arrangement of multiple pivots to convert a large motion into a small one, with corresponding multiplication of cutting force.

How to Use: **1. Select a bolt cutter whose jaws will fit around the object to be cut.**

2. Open the cutter's jaws by spreading its handles. Fit the object to be cut as deep as possible into the jaws.

3. Close the cutter's handles firmly together.

Tool-Kit Minimum:	People who habitually lose keys to padlocks need a pair of bolt cutters.

---

123. **BOOSTER CABLE**

General Description:	*A coil of flexible insulated wire with four metal spring clamps attached to it.* Booster cable is not a single wire but a pair of thick ones stuck together. Two of the clamps are colored red and two of them are black; the red ones are marked with plus signs and the letters POS while the black ones are marked with minus signs and NEG. The jaws of all four clamps have metal teeth.

The car has a battery for starting and for running its electrical gear. Leaving the headlights on overnight can discharge the battery, and in the morning the car won't start. Booster cables, also called "jumper cables," allow you to start the car from the electrical system of a separate, working car. Most of the time, the discharged battery will come back to life. You can also use booster cables to start a car that has a completely dead battery or even a missing one.

Habitat: Trunk of car. Sold by hardware stores, home centers, and auto parts stores.

Primary Use: Starting a car whose battery has been discharged.

Operating Principle: Car batteries have a positive (+) and a negative (–) terminal and booster cables have to be connected the right way. On all American cars made since 1955, and European and Asian cars made since 1971, the battery's negative terminal connects directly to the metal of the car body and engine block. The car is said to have a negative ground. Negative terminals are likely to be colored black or to wear a black plastic cover, while positive ones wear red.

Variations: Booster cables come in lengths ranging from 6 feet (2 m) to 16 feet (5 m), and in thicknesses of 8 gauge (16 mm) and 10 gauge (25 mm).

Safety Note: Car batteries are dangerous: They contain sulphuric acid, emit hydrogen gas, and pack a huge electrical charge. It's rare but possible for hydrogen discharged from the battery to ignite and cause a small explosion, spraying battery acid.

Reduce the risks by connecting the cables in the order discussed in Steps 3 through 5 below. Wear safety glasses. If any battery acid spills or sprays in your eyes, immediately wash them in running water and get medical attention.

If battery acid gets on your skin, dilute it with running water and then wash with soap. If it splashes on clothing, wash the clothing as soon as possible. Wash your hands after touching the battery.

How to Use: 1. **Park the working car close to the dead one, but make sure they are not touching. Shut both cars off and open their engine hoods.**

2. **Put on your safety glasses. Gather all four cable clamps in your hand so they don't dangle and accidentally touch either car.**

3. **Locate the positive terminal on the battery in the dead car. Sometimes it's on the top, sometimes on the side, and some cars have a concealed battery with a remote positive under the hood, marked with a + sign and a red plastic cap. Push the cap aside and connect one of the red cable clamps to the terminal. Wiggle the clamp to make its teeth bite.**

4. **Connect the other red clamp to the positive terminal in the working car. Connect one of the black (–) clamps to the negative terminal of the working battery.**

5. **Start the good car and let it idle.**

6. **Connect the remaining black clamp to the engine block or metal bumper of the stalled car, not to its negative battery terminal.**

7. **Wait several minutes while charge transfers between the batteries. Then start the dead car.**

8. **Let the cars idle together for a few minutes. Shut off the good car and disconnect the cables in reverse order—Step 6, then Step 4, then Step 3.**

9. **Let the newly started car run for at least 30 minutes, preferably an hour, before turning it off, to ensure the battery charges fully.**

Tool-Kit
Minimum: Every car should have a set of booster cables coiled neatly in the trunk.

---

124. **BOX WRENCH**

General
Description: *A flat bar of shiny steel that flares to a U-shaped opening on one end, with a round eye on the other.* The round

eye has the corners of a 12-sided shape pressed into it, and the steel bar bends upward just behind it. The U-shaped end bends about the same amount to one side. There's a number stamped into the metal near both ends indicating the size of nuts and bolts the wrench was designed to fit.

Habitat:
Toolbox of mechanic and handyperson. Sold by hardware stores and auto parts stores. Though available singly, box wrenches often are sold in sets intended to cover a full range of sizes, are usually found in groups, and often must be used in pairs.

Primary Use:
Loosening or tightening square and hexagonal nuts and bolts.

Operating Principle:
The wrench is a lever that concentrates turning force on the nut or bolt. The small amount of crank in its handle, along with the 12 points in its closed end, help the operator reach inaccessible fittings and make partial turns.

Variations:
Wrenches are manufactured for every size nut and bolt, in both American and metric increments of measure. In general, larger wrenches are also longer.

How to Use: 1.
Choose a wrench that precisely fits the part you want to tighten or loosen. In many situations you will need two wrenches, one on the head of the bolt and the

other on the nut. They're usually, but not necessarily, the same size.

2.   **Recall that nuts and bolts tighten when turned clockwise; determine where to fit the wrench and settle it there.**

3.   **Push or tug on the wrench to turn the part in the desired direction. When you run out of handle room, lift and reseat the wrench (it might help to also turn it over) and resume.**

Tool-Kit Minimum: A set of eight or more box wrenches sized in ¹/₁₆-inch (or 1 mm) increments.

125a–c.   **CENTER PUNCH**

General Description: *A round or hexagonal bar of steel about as thick as an adult finger and only a bit longer, with one end sloping to a broad point.* The other end is flat, or if the punch is old, mushroomed over from hammering.

Habitat: Toolbox of mechanic, metalworker, or handyperson. Sold by hardware stores and home centers. The broad point identifies the center punch; if you were to measure the point, the included angle would be somewhere between 60 and 90 degrees. It also distinguishes the center punch from the awl, which has a long tapered point; from the drift, which has a flat end instead of a point; and from the nail set, whose end is not just flat but also dimpled.

Primary Use:	Making a dimple in the workpiece (either wood or metal) when struck lightly with a hammer, in order to indicate a dimension or start a drill.
Secondary Uses:	Marking the screw centers for a hinge. Making a witness mark to show how parts should fit together. Driving small metal parts out of holes.
Operating Principle:	When struck with a hammer, the mass of the center punch transmits energy to its point.
Variations:	Some center punches have a tapered shank, while others have a straight shank.
How to Use:	1. **Carefully locate the spot where you want a punch mark.**
	2. **Set the point of the punch on the mark**
	3. **Tap the head of the punch with a hammer.**
	4. **Lift the punch and see if the dimple is deep enough. If not, repeat Step 2.**

126. 📷   **COLD CHISEL**

General
Description: *A round, square, or hexagonal bar of iron that's about as*
thick as an adult finger and twice as long; one end grad-
ually tapers, then slopes to make a sharp beveled edge.
The other end, called the "head," is flat or, on an old
chisel, somewhat mushroomed over.

Habitat: Toolbox or workshop of mechanic, metalworker,
plumber, or handyperson. Sold by hardware stores
and home centers. The metal bar or shank without an
additional handle distinguishes the cold chisel from
similar wood chisels, which feature wood or plastic
handles.

Primary
Use: Cutting metal. Cutting notches and grooves in metal.
Removing burrs and lumps off metal.

Variations: Mason's chisels have a wide cutting edge and are for
cutting brick and hardened mortar.

Safety Note: Wear safety glasses and work gloves when hammering
a cold chisel. Repeated hammer blows may make the
head flare into a mushroom shape, which might split
and shed flying shrapnel.

How to Use: 1.   **The metal you plan to cut has to be held in a vise**
(page 235) or clamped to something massive and
sturdy.

2. **Wear safety glasses and work gloves. Hold the chisel in your fist like a dagger, with its sharp edge emerging from the little finger side, not the thumb side. If your hammer aim is uncertain, hold the chisel with locking pliers (page 259).**

3. **Set the edge of the chisel on the edge of the metal where you want to cut.**

4. **Strike the head of the chisel with a heavy hammer. Repeat until you achieve the desired results.**

5. **Use a file to clean up the cut edges.**

Tool-Kit Minimum: For the handyperson who cuts metal often, one cold chisel is a necessity.

127. **CREEPER**

General Description: *A flat wooden panel with a low cushion near one edge.* There's an odd sort of tilted wheel at each corner of a creeper, mounted on bent axles. Standing on end, the creeper is about waist high. Flat on the ground, it's no higher than the top of your foot. When flat on the ground, a push sends it rolling in any direction—those wheels pivot easily and turn freely.

Mechanics lie on the creeper and, propelled by foot power, roll underneath cars to work on them.

Most cars are so low to the ground that they have to be up on jack stands (page 289) before there's room for the mechanic; most light trucks are already high enough and don't need to be jacked onto stands.

Habitat: Garage or tool cabinet of Sunday mechanic. Sold by auto parts stores.

Primary Use: Rolling the mechanic underneath the vehicle to work on it.

Secondary Use: A flatbed hand truck for moving equipment and appliances up to about 300 pounds. Compared to regular hand trucks and dollies, the advantage of the creeper is that the object to be moved does not have to be lifted very high.

Variations: Mechanics often sit on an armless office chair set low to the ground when working on vehicles and machines.

Safety Note: Do not use a creeper underneath cars lifted on a regular tire-changing jack, which is not stable. You risk the car slipping off the jack and falling on your body.

How to Use: 1. **Check that the creeper's wheels turn freely, then place it flat on the ground.**

2. **Be sure the vehicle rests securely on jack stands, with chocks on both sides of all the wheels on the ground.**

3. **Find the tools you expect to need and put them in a tray or on the ground alongside the vehicle, where you will be able to reach them. Set up a bright work light.**

4. **Sit on the creeper, on the end with no cushion. Lie back so your head rests on the cushion. Get comfortable.**

5. **Propel yourself with a combination of hands on the vehicle, plus heel action on the ground. Keep your hands near your face to help you avoid a painful bump against some part of the vehicle.**

6. **When done, reverse Steps 5 and 4.**

Tool-Kit Minimum:
Only the most die-hard weekend car tinkerers need one.

128a–e.

FILE

General Description:
A flat bar of iron with a handle on one end and a tight pattern of grooves (called "teeth") cut into the surface. Removing the handle exposes the pointed end of the file (called the "tang").

Files are described by their length (which can range from the width of the hand up to the forearm from elbow to fingertips); their cross-section (flat, half round, round, triangular), the coarseness of their teeth (fine, second-cut, coarse, bastard), and whether they have a single set of teeth (mill files) or two sets crossing one another (machine or double-cut files). Fine and second-cut teeth are for removing scratches and burrs and creating a smooth finish on metal. Coarse and bastard teeth shape and fit metal parts and smooth wooden ones. Rasps (page 218) are extremely coarse files for removing a lot of wood in a hurry.

Habitat: Toolbox of metalworker, woodworker, or mechanic. Sold by hardware stores and home centers. The tight teeth cut into their surfaces distinguish files from other, similarly shaped tools. Files usually are found in groups along with a file card: a flat, two-sided brush for cleaning their teeth.

Primary Uses: Shaping and smoothing metal parts. Removing burrs.

Secondary Uses: Sharpening such tools as lawn mowers, axes, and hedge shears.

Variations: Jewelers use sets of short, slender files (called "needle files"). Triangular files sharpen the teeth of handsaws, while round files the size of a pencil are for sharpening chain saws. Shaped files (half round for example) can create or finish any shapes they'll fit into.

Safety Note: Files without handles are a safety hazard and should not be used. The risk is that the file's teeth catch on the workpiece, driving the tang into the operator's hand. File handles are easy to transfer from one file to another, and some handles are made with an adjustable opening specifically so they can be switched around.

How to Use: 1. **The file is a two-handed tool. Always trap the workpiece in a vise (page 235) or clamp it to the workbench (page 237).**

2. **Wear work gloves and be sure the file handle is seated firmly on the tang. To seat the handle, hold the file upright with the handle uppermost and bang its square end straight down onto the workbench.**

3. **Take a stable marching stance. Hold the file handle in one hand and grasp its other end between thumb and fingers.**

4. **The file cuts on the push stroke. Push the file across the workpiece, then lift it for each return stroke.**

5. **Keep the file teeth clean. Brush them with the wire side of the file card.**

Tool-Kit Minimum: An 8-inch (20 cm) fine mill file, plus a 10-inch (25 cm) double-cut bastard file.

129. 📷   **HACKSAW**

General
Description:

A metal frame about as long as your forearm and as wide as your hand, with a narrow saw blade on one long side and a pistol-grip handle at one end. The saw-blade is thin and no wider than a fingernail, with extremely small and fine teeth that point away from the handle. A hole on each end of the blade fits over a pin mounted on the frame. There's a thumbscrew for loosening and tightening the blade. The blade-mounting fittings can be turned so the blade operates at right-angles to the saw frame.

The hacksaw is for cutting metal. Turning the blade in the frame allows the saw to make deeper cuts or to reach farther into the workpiece without inter-ference by the frame. The many tiny teeth tend to heat and to clog with metal chips; cool and lubricate the action and float the chips with periodic squirts of cutting oil or light machine oil.

Habitat:

Mechanic's toolbox and truck of builder or plumber. Sold by hardware stores and home centers. The ten-sionable frame, with the long and narrow blade, is characteristic of hacksaws; the coping saw (page 197) has a shorter blade and a lighter frame.

Primary
Use:

Sawing all kinds of metal and plastic. In movies, cut-ting through jail bars.

Operating Principle: Tension on the saw blade allows it to exert enough force without bending or buckling.

Variations: Newer hacksaws have a cam and lever mechanism for putting more tension on the blade than is possible with the older screw mechanism. Short hacksaws for working in tight spaces have a protruding blade.

How to Use: 1. **Make a layout line on the work and secure it in a vise (page 235) or clamp it to the workbench (page 237). Wear your work gloves.**

2. **Start the saw with short, light, one-handed strokes. Brace the blade with the gloved thumb of your other hand to keep it on the layout line.**

3. **Once the saw has made a groove in the metal, steer the saw and increase the cutting force by shifting your free hand to the far end of the saw frame. Take long strokes using the full length of the blade. Lift the blade on each return stroke.**

4. **Periodically flood the cutting zone with light oil to cool the blade and float the chips.**

5. **To cut thin metal such as a piece of angle iron, tilt the saw frame so the blade meets the work at a shallow angle—this increases the number of teeth working on the metal.**

6. **To cut sheet metal, use snips (page 294), or sandwich the workpiece between two pieces of wood and saw through wood and metal.**

Tool-Kit
Minimum:

A standard hacksaw with a can of cutting oil and several blades.

---

130. 📷 **HEX WRENCH**

General
Description:

A black bar of metal, not as long as your hand, with a right-angle bent like the letter L. The metal is hexagonal in cross-section and about the diameter of a pencil or smaller. The ends of the bar are finished straight across. The hex wrench or hex key, also called an "Allen wrench," fits the six-sided socket on top of machine screws, which are very common on machinery. American hex wrenches are made in many sizes, each 1/64-inch larger than the one before. Metric hex wrenches are graduated in half millimeters.

Habitat:

Toolbox of mechanic, builder, or handyperson. Sold by hardware stores, home centers, and auto parts stores. Often comes included in "some assembly required" furniture. The hexagonal cross-section and right-angle bend are characteristic.

Primary
Use:

Tightening and loosening hexagonal socket-head machine screws and bolts.

Variations: Both American and metric hex wrenches come in sets of common sizes folded into a handle, like a pocket knife. Ball drivers are hex wrenches with a hexagonal ball formed on the long end, which helps reach inaccessible screws by permitting misalignment.

How to Use: 1. **Choose a hex wrench that exactly fits the recess in the top of the screw head. "Close" isn't close enough: the fit has to be exact.**

2. **Fit the short end of the hex wrench into the socket on the screw head and push or pull the hex wrench in the direction you want to turn the screw (clockwise tightens, counterclockwise loosens).**

3. **Once the screw is loose, switch to the long end of the hex wrench and spin it between your fingers.**

Tool-Kit Minimum: If you ever work on machinery, you'll need two sets of hex wrenches, one American and the other metric.

131. **JACK STANDS**

General Description: *A heavy, four-sided metal base with a stout iron stanchion rising out of it; the top of the stanchion has a saddle like a shallow U.* There's a series of holes in the apparatus, with a pin or "dog" you can use to lock the stanchion in place over a range of heights. It's knee-high at its highest position and half that at its lowest.

A pair of jack stands is the Sunday mechanic's auto hoist. While all cars come with a tire-changing jack, they are prone to slip, and it is not safe to work underneath a car resting on one. Use the jack to lift one end of the car onto the jack stands and let it rest there. If the stands are on solid, flat ground, and provided you chock the wheels of the car, it will be safe to work underneath.

Habitat:
Mechanic's garage or car trunk. Sold by hardware stores, home centers, and auto parts stores. Jack stands are always sold and used in pairs.

Primary
Use:
Safely holding one end of a car off the ground so the handyperson can work underneath it.

Secondary
Uses:
Jack stands and a good auto jack can be used to lift and reposition other heavy objects.

Operating
Principle:
A four-sided stand with a centered stanchion makes a stable platform so long as it's not hit with sideways forces. This is why a car on jack stands still needs to have its wheels chocked so it cannot roll.

Variations:
Some jack stands are fixed in height and are not adjustable. Some have a three-sided base. Some Sunday mechanics prefer to lift the car by driving it onto a matched pair of ramps.

How to Use: 1. **Use jack stands made for automotive use. Jury-rigged substitutes, such as stacks of concrete blocks, aren't stable or safe.**

2. **Chock both sides of the two wheels that will remain on the ground.**

3. **Check the owner's manual to locate the car's jack and its jack points under the chassis. Fit the jack under one of the jack points and use it to lift one corner of the car.**

4. **Fit the jack stand under the raised axle, as close to the wheel as you can get it. Lower the jack to lower the car onto the jack stand.**

5. **Go to the other side of the car and repeat Steps 3 and 4.**

6. **With the jack removed, check the wheel chocks, and try really hard to wiggle the car on the stands. If it's going to slip off, be sure that happens before you crawl underneath.**

7. **When you want to let the car down, use the jack to lift it off first one stand, then the other. Remember to remove the wheel chocks before you drive away.**

132a–c.   **LOCKING PLIERS**

General
Description:

*A metal contraption with two handles and two short
jaws, featuring a knurled screw coming out of one handle and a toggle, a kind of shadow handle, inside the
other.* Locking pliers seem to have three pivot points
with a bar of metal bridging between the handles.
There's also a spring visible between the handles.

Adjustable locking pliers amplify and armor the
pincer grip of thumb and forefinger. Turning the
knurled knob adjusts the opening between the jaws,
whose grip is inflexible and unbreakable once they
have been squeezed onto the workpiece; pressing the
toggle between the handles releases the jaws.

Habitat:

Toolbox of mechanic, builder, or plumber. Sold by
hardware stores and home centers. The presence of
the triple-pivot and handle controls identify adjustable locking pliers.

Primary
Use:

Putting the death grip on a metal part in order to pull
it, tighten it, loosen it, twist it, or bend it.

Secondary
Uses:

In the event that a copper water pipe breaks in your
house and you can't locate the shutoff valve,
adjustable locking pliers are the only tool that can
save you. Cut the pipe with a tubing cutter (page
269) or hacksaw (page 286), then use locking pliers
to squeeze the end flat, bend it back on itself, and roll

it up like a croissant.

When you've suffered a flat tire in the dead of winter and find yourself without a tire wrench, grab tight with locking pliers, stand on the handle, and thrust your weight downward; for extra leverage fit a large box wrench (page 276) or a length of iron pipe over the pliers' handle. In medical emergencies, locking pliers can help extract fishhooks, teeth, bullets, and arrows.

Operating Principle:
The triple-knuckle arrangement converts a large amount of handle motion into a small amount of jaw motion, with a corresponding increase in the power of the squeeze.

Variations:
Adjustable locking pliers are manufactured with many jaw styles, including needlenose, chain, and clamping.

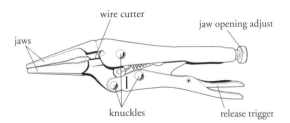

jaws — wire cutter — jaw opening adjust — knuckles — release trigger

How to Use: 1.
Choose pliers whose jaw shape and opening range matches the fitting you intend to wrestle.

2. **Turn the jaw-adjusting screw until the jaws make the best possible fit on the part. Twisting clockwise tightens most fittings, so orient the pliers for the action you want. Squeeze the handles together until they click tight.**

3. **Pull, bend, or twist the handle of the pliers until the part is persuaded to follow.**

4. **To release the pliers, press the toggle inside the handles.**

Tool-Kit   One large pair of adjustable locking pliers, plus one
Minimum: small, needlenose locking pliers.

133a–d.   **SNIPS**

General   *Lengths of metal crossed at a pivot with long handles*
Description: *and stout, finger-length blades.* Like scissors, the sharp
edges of snips slide tightly past one another until the
handles come together and stop the action. Snips are
for powering through tough materials such as sheet
metal, leather, dense textiles, and heavy plastic. Unlike
scissors, some snips have a return spring to open them
for the next bite. Compound-action snips (aircraft
snips) have a double knuckle for extra leverage, with a
curving blade that slices all along its length.

Habitat: Toolbox of mechanic, builder, or handyperson. Sold by hardware stores and home centers. Distinguish snips from scissors by their larger handles and shorter blades; distinguish them from bolt cutters by their bypass blades.

Primary Use: Cutting sheet metal and other tough sheet materials. Cutting hardware cloth, wire mesh, and window screen.

Variations: There are custom snips for every metal—aluminum, copper, iron, and steel—and most other materials including leather, wood veneer, meat, and flowers.

How to Use: 1. **Draw or scratch a layout line on the material.**

2. **Hold the snips in your dominant hand and open the jaws.**

3. **Hold the material in your other hand and feed it as far as possible into the jaws.**

4. **Close the snips on the material.**

5. **Open the snips and repeat Steps 3 and 4.**

Note: **When possible, choose snips that are meant for the material; most snips will make some kind of cut in most sheet materials.**

Tool-Kit
Minimum:

One general-purpose shop snips or tin snips with comfortable handles and short, sharp blades.

134a–b.

SOCKET WRENCH

General
Description:

A shiny steel handle not much longer than a hand span, with a round end that has a square stud coming out of it. Opposite the square stud on a socket wrench is a button and a small toggle. If you turn the stud it makes a clicking sound, but it only goes one way. When you flip the small toggle, the stud is able to turn the other way but loses the ability to turn the way it did at first.

The socket wrench is an ingenious solution to the problem of having box wrenches in every conceivable size, as well as to the problem of getting access to hard-to-reach nuts and bolts.

A flock of sockets always accompanies the socket wrench. They're hollow steel cylinders with a square, stud-sized hole in one end and a 12-pointed opening in the other. A socket fits onto the square stud; pushing the button on the wrench operates a concealed ball-bearing latch that locks the socket in place. The 12-pointed opening fits onto the head of a nut or a bolt. For a different sized nut, swap sockets, which are available in both American and metric sizes.

The geometry of the wrench helps solve the problem of access. With a regular box wrench, there has to be room to maneuver the handle in the same plane as the nut or bolt, where other fittings are certain to interfere. The socket lifts the handle of the wrench off the plane of the nut. If that's not enough, socket wrenches also have numerous extensions and U-joint fittings for improving access and gaining clearance to swing the handle.

Habitat:
Toolbox of mechanic and general handyperson. Sold by hardware stores, home centers, and auto parts stores. The configuration of the socket wrench—straight handle with a square stud at one end—is characteristic, as are the cylindrical sockets that accompany the wrench.

Primary Uses:
Tightening and loosening nuts and bolts. Tightening and loosening any square or hexagonal fitting a socket can accommodate.

Operating Principle:
If you can get a socket onto the nut or bolt, you'll be able to connect it via extensions and U-joints to a socket wrench. The long handle provides leverage for turning the fitting.

Variations:
Socket wrenches are known by the size of the stud that fits their sockets. Adapters make it possible to use smaller sockets with larger wrenches, though not the other way around.

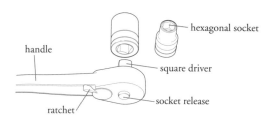

handle

hexagonal socket

square driver

socket release

ratchet

How to Use: **1.** **Fit the socket onto the socket wrench and fit it onto the nut, bolt, or fitting. If it won't reach, add extensions and U-joints as needed.**

2. **Flip the toggle on the socket wrench so it exerts force in the desired direction (clockwise tightens). It will click and turn freely in the other direction.**

3. **Push or pull the handle of the wrench to turn the fitting. The clicking ratchet allows you to swing the handle back and continue turning the fitting without removing the wrench.**

Tool-Kit Minimum: One 3/8-inch (10 mm) socket wrench with a set of sockets and basic extensions.

 135a–b.

TIRE GAUGE

General Description: *A chrome cylinder the size of a pen with a ball on one end and a square white plug sticking out the other.* Tire gauges often have a pen-style pocket clip. The ball has a little round stud on one side, and a large round opening on the other. If you pull the square white plug out of the cylinder, it's got numbers and a graduated scale on it.

The tire gauge is for measuring air pressure in car and truck tires. The round stud is for releasing air from a standard tire valve; the round opening fits over a standard tire valve; and the square plug is a scale marked in pounds per square inch as well as in kilopascals, the equivalent metric measure.

Habitat:	Car glove box and mechanic's toolbox. Sold by hardware stores and auto parts stores. The round opening for the tire valve is characteristic though the sliding scale is not, since some gauges have a dial instead.
Primary Use:	Measuring air pressure in vehicle tires.
Variations:	Some tire gauges have a dial readout, and some are now digital. Some have a hose between gauge and valve, which makes them easier to read.
How to Use: 1.	**Check air pressure when the tires are cold. Driving heats the tires and may give a false reading.**
2.	**Remove the valve cap from the tire.**

3. Plug the gauge onto the valve stem and press it on tight. If you hear the hiss of escaping air, it's not seated correctly; reorient it and try again.

4. Read the numbers on the graduated rod. The last number you can see is the tire pressure.

5. Compare the reading with the sticker containing tire pressure information mounted on the jamb that becomes visible when you open the driver's door.

6. Add or release air to bring the tire pressure to the recommended value. If the sticker gives a range of pressures, choose the higher number. Make sure the tire pressure is the same in both front tires and in both rear tires. Unbalanced pressure causes premature tire wear and may affect how the car handles.

Tool-Kit Minimum: Every car needs its own tire pressure gauge.

136. **TIRE WRENCH**

General Description: *Two bars of iron crossed in the middle and joined together there, forming a cross.* A tire wrench is about knee-high if you stand it up on end. There's a socket on each of the four arms, and all have hexagonal openings, but they're not all the same size.

The tire wrench, lug wrench, or tire star is for removing the lug nuts that hold the wheels on your car. One of those hexagonal sockets will fit your car's lug nuts. Changing tires on the roadside can be difficult because the lug nuts were originally tightened more than necessary with an air-powered wrench. The little take-apart wrench that came with the car isn't up to the job.

Habitat: Mechanic's toolbox, garage, or trunk of car. Sold by auto parts stores.

Primary Use: Loosening and tightening lug nuts on automotive wheels.

Operating Principle: Unlike other wrenches, the lug wrench allows you to increase leverage by both pushing and pulling.

How to Use: 1. **Begin the process while the car is still on the ground, which keeps the wheel from turning.**

2. **Choose the socket that best fits the lug nuts on your car. Recall that turning counterclockwise loosens nuts; clockwise tightens them.**

3. **Fit the socket onto one of the lug nuts. Then take a stable stance and grip the lug wrench with both hands, one hand on each of the two sideways-projecting branches.**

4. Lift hard on one side of the wrench while pushing just as hard on the other side. Grunting helps, and so does leaning into it to apply your full body weight.

5. When the lug nut lets go, usually with a sharp screech, leave it and move on to the next nut.

6. When all of the lug nuts have released their grip, jack up the car following the advice in your owner's manual. Then spin the nuts off their studs and change the wheel.

7. To retighten the wheel, reverse Steps 6 through 4. Do the final tightening with the wheel resting on the ground, off the jack. Tighten the lug nuts by moving across the wheel from one to another, not around it.

Tool-Kit Minimum: Whenever you acquire a new car, check whether the wheel lugs are American or metric, and buy the car its own lug wrench. It's cheap emergency insurance.

Index

Numbers in **bold** (for example, **11**) are tool numbers, and can be used to locate tools in the photograph section. All other numbers are page numbers.